FROM OPPRESSION TO FREEDOM

Intercultural Research Series of Anthropography No. 4

FROM OPPRESSION TO FREEDOM:

A Study of the Kaivani Gnostics

KEVIN SHEPHERD

Anthropographia Publications
Cambridge

First published in 1988
by Anthropographia Publications,
P.O. Box 13, Cambridge CB4 1EZ.

ISBN 0 9508680 4 3

Printed in Great Britain by
Redwood Burn Limited, Trowbridge, Wiltshire.

CONTENTS

PREFACE

The two parts of this book may be read as self-contained sections, though I have attempted to indicate the connections between them. The Kaivani episodes are little known to a general readership, and much data has hitherto been disconnected in scholarly literature. The Kaivani phenomenon is part of the older tradition known as *ishraq* (illuminism), an Iranian experiential philosophy which has had strong repercussions in India.

This book is part of a series arising from the research strategy of anthropography, the term designating my recently formulated polymathic science of the human entity (*anthropos*), a science which encompasses the dimensions of both history and meaning in its worldview.

Kevin R.D. Shepherd

Intercultural Research Centre of Anthropography,
Cambridge.

October 1985.

PART ONE:

THE LIFE OF A DERVISH

In reporting matters of a deeper nature than the mundane, it is often necessary to explain a thing in conjunction with several others, since all may be vitally interconnected. Nobody wants only one piece of a jig-saw puzzle.

An early Aryan religion was that now known as Zoroastrianism, after the prophet Zoroaster. The name is not strictly accurate, since it is an hellenicized version of the Persian Zarathushtra. These orthographical variants are paralleled perhaps by dating disparities. Differing authorities have placed him as far apart in time as *circa* 600 B.C. and *c.* 1500 B.C., and the question of chronology is still being debated by scholars. The scarcity of historical information is perhaps inevitable when one considers the subsequent cultural changes in Iran, eventually resulting in a minority group of Zoroastrians. The religion has been described as a museum piece, though it is probably no more so than several others. Very little is known with certainty about the putative founder's teaching perspective; the famous *Gathas* are often obscure, while other literary sources preserving his doctrine are of a much later date.

Any biographical presentation of this ancient prophet amounts to a very shadowy outline. His geographical background is still in dispute. The traditions have it that he was thirty when he began his role of prophethood, but this is probably a symbolic number. Zarathushtra encountered opposition in his home territory, and for several years his only pupil was his cousin Maidhyoimanha. Later he moved elsewhere, to a scholastically uncertain territory where a local king known as Vishtaspa became his patron. Some late traditions connect this monarch with Balkh, in Central Asia, but this is questionable.

Zarathushtra's fundamental triple precept of good thought, good word, and good deed is widely known, but remains a fragmentary introduction to an obscured code. The Gathas are hymns attributed to him, but these present severe linguistic difficulties to scholars of the subject, and different translations are marked by their wide variations.

To what extent the subsequent Zoroastrian religion of Iran was a continuation of Zarathushtra's teaching is a matter of dispute. It was at a much later date that the

Sassanian dynasty of Iran feuded with the Byzantine empire. Yet both of these persecution zones fell substantially in status before a new cultural impulse from a totally unexpected quarter.

The ancient world was accustomed to thinking of Arabia largely as a mort of disunited Bedouin tribes, primitive vassals of the Sassanians, conveniently off the beaten track of civilization. Yet Muhammad imparted a new and powerful unity to a thousand tribes in a single decade during the early seventh century, though only after he and his early associates had undergone much persecution. He has been described as the first nation-builder to achieve complete fulfilment prior to decease. Owing to this unique achievement he did in effect become the emperor of Arabia, though he never proclaimed himself as such. He preferred to mend his own clothes, repair his shoes, and sweep out his own house. He effectively stopped the drunkenness and immorality which until then had sapped Arab achievements. In addition to the codes of religious and civic law he provided, Muhammad told his compatriots that Moses and Jesus had been part of a continuing programme of revelation which had been at work, and that: "There is not a nation but a messenger passed among them" (*Quran*, surah 35, v.24).

It was not long before Islamic civilization covered a substantial portion of the globe from Spain to India. Victorian ideas of a religion of the sword should no longer exist in view of historical research, any more than modern materialists should regard Christianity entirely as the religion of inquisition. Indoctrination of mere belief will always produce incongruities. Lack of intelligence, or sheer laziness to learn, is a fault unhappily not restricted to the religious sphere. The majority of the modern Western population are not conversant with the theories of Einstein or Sperry, despite the fact that they are all nominally civilized moderns. The general belief code might be expressed in the lofty formula: "I have a will of my own and must enjoy myself."

The Arab conquest of Iran and other countries was largely bloodless. Many vassals welcomed a change of rulership, and official tolerance was accorded to all "people of a book" who were believers in prophetic religion according to the monotheist concept. Forcible conversion was not the rule, and as a consequence, it took three centuries before the Iranian majority were assimilated to Islam. The Zoroastrians had a lower status than that of Jews or Christians, and official Arab policy was one of aloof contempt, though there were some Muslims who were eager to proselytize, including some of the converts from Zoroastrianism, ironically enough. Though not persecuted, the non-Muslims were restricted socially and economically, and in many cases it appears to have been this underdog status which contributed to the change of religion in Iran. The Arabs took over the Sassanian taxation system, with its land-tax and poll-tax, the latter identified with the Arabic *jizya*. This *jizya* was made into a special tax on unbelievers. Yet the word *jizya* occurs only once in the *Quran* (surah 9, v.29), and does not there carry a legal meaning. It has been thought that the original context of such terms was forgotten by the time historians recorded Quranic events, which they interpreted in the light of later conditions and events (Hitti, p. 171).

Minority involvement was another matter. In the early seventh century a Zoroastrian known as Salman-i Farsi ("the Persian") is reported to have travelled to Medina, the Arabian stronghold of the Prophet Muhammad. Salman is reputedly the first Iranian to have become a Muslim, and one of the few Muslims to have assimilated the more esoteric aspect of Muhammad's ideas. The life of Salman-i Farsi is told in diverse versions in both sunni and shia sources. It appears that Salman became a close companion of Ali, the assassinated fourth Caliph; Salman himself became the governor of Mada'in but continued to live in simplicity, a characteristic of the early Muslims. Salman died at Mada'in in 655–6; the Iranian scholar S.H. Nasr has described him as being among the foremost of the early sufis.

Another of the most famous of the early Persian sufis was Abu Yazid al-Bistami (d.*c.*874). His grandfather was a Zoroastrian, but the family subsequently became Muslims, and his father was a leading citizen of Bistam, a town in the province of Khorasan. He may have travelled as far as Sind in north-west India to become the disciple of Abu Ali, regarded as highly unorthodox because he did not perform the daily prayer observances of Islam. Abu Yazid, better known as Bayazid, became an exponent of the gnostic trend of "intoxication" teaching; he is reported to have repeatedly put on a rough girdle of the type compulsory for non-Muslims. Such details were later incorporated in the biographies in what was arguably a piecemeal form, making it difficult to see the full context of events. Bayazid may have been urging that one is not a true Muslim unless and until an inner regeneration replaces belief observance. A facile belief observance was shared alike by the increasingly opulent court and the increasingly dogmatic legists and divines, not to mention the many Zoroastrians who found worldly advancement easier via a change of religion.

One of those in affinity with the Bistami tradition of Khorasan was Abu'l Mughith al-Hallaj (d.922), whose father was a Zoroastrian convert to Islam. He travelled widely between Makkah (Mecca) and Turkestan, emphasized the importance of Jesus as an apocalyptic figurehead, and was acquainted with Greek philosophy. He was finally active in Baghdad. Here in the early tenth century, near the ruins of Babylon and Ctesiphon (the Sassanian capital), he was condemned to death on grounds of heresy. The incident is one of the most well known in sufi annals, and has become something of a commonplace anecdote, and one suffering from hindsight in some respects.

Al-Hallaj was not committed to judicial butchery merely because he had stated "*Ana'l-Haqq*" (I am the Truth). Nor was it simply that he was accused of being a secret Christian, and an opponent of the Makkah pilgrimage, since he was of the view that the pilgrimage could be performed anywhere providing the correct inner dedication was made. Possibly his major sin was to criticize the economic policy of the Baghdad court. He was not merely a threat to officialdom and orthodoxy, but also to sufi imposters like Ghulam Khalil. (Imposters are proverbial in sufi lore, though both traditionalist and modernist studies of the sufi phenomenon tend to ignore this etic qualification, which accordingly produces some very confusing accounts for the unwary). Ghulam Khalil is reported by Hujwiri to have gained influence with the Caliph before whom he maligned sufi figureheads in Baghdad, since he desired their banishment from the city so that his own influence would reign supreme. This schemer nearly caused the death of half a dozen leading members of the Baghdad sufi "school," including Abu Hamza, Nuri, Somnun, and Junayd. If we can believe Attar's report, all these men were actually brought before the Caliph while in the presence of an executioner (though Qushayri says that Junayd escaped the court owing to his juristic affiliations). That they were all acquitted may seem an anti-climax, but it must have been a relief to those involved, even if they were mystics as committed as Hallaj was to the cause of social metamorphosis.

When pressure was later focussed upon the outspoken Hallaj, the detractors achieved success. A group of theologians made a determined attempt to dispense with the heretic, concocting a suitable indictment (which Attar credibly says was garbled) that was presented to the Caliph. But treasury officials and viziers with pet fiscal policies were notably amongst his opponents, and his desire for moral reform was undoubtedly anathema to them. Influential courtiers rigged a political accusation after Hallaj had gained a lengthy imprisonment. There are indications that the Caliph was reluctant to kill him, but a hostile vizier pressed Al-Muqtadir into signing a death warrant.

When Hallaj was led in chains to the scaffold, it was to meet a savage execution, the details of which it is better to spare those readers who do not share the sadistic tendencies of readers of some modern literature.

While it has frequently been ignored that several of the followers of Hallaj were executed in Baghdad a few years after his death, it is legitimate to wonder how much else was omitted from both traditional reports and more recent scholarly surveys. One of the figures who has perhaps rarely been viewed in accurate perspective was the reputed leader of the Baghdad sufis, namely Abu'l Qasim al-Junayd (d.910), a Persian whose ancestors came from the ancient town of Nihavand in Iran. He and his associates were under public accusation of being infidels and atheists; he appears to have pushed further developments undercover, and made his teaching compatible with the *sunna,* the standard Islamic code expressed in the *hadith* or traditions of the Prophet. He lived as a silk merchant, and the proceeds of his trade were used to help many others who lived an ascetic life. His house in Baghdad was a centre for local *dervish* types, and those from other countries who were continually passing through the capital. He remained on good terms with the orthodox, being an accomplished scholar in jurisprudence and theology, and scrupulously conforming to the *sharia* (religious practise). He refused to teach in public, was allegedly highly selective concerning pupils, and worded all his correspondence extremely cautiously. He strictly discountenanced expressions of gnosis that might be considered extravagant by the literalists, the reason for his notable aloofness towards Hallaj.

Junayd's demonstration of "sobriety" has for long been contrasted with that of the "intoxication" principle associated with Hallaj. This is arguably an error in the simplified versions which have maintained the hidebound notions that are the preserve of nominal sufis.

The preservation method of unorthodox thinkers was more effective in some areas than others, but possibly the worst factor they had to deal with was not the fanatical religionists, but the imitators who imagined that they were "sufis" and who accordingly declared themselves as such.

Scholars have debated at length upon the origin of the word *sufi*, and I do not intend here to participate in this futile discussion. What has been called the "Baghdad school" of Junayd's day was known to contemporaries as *arbab at-tauhid* ("people of *tauhid*"), though *tauhid* was here a technical term much more intricate than the standard religious idea of the "unity of God." For Junayd and his group the term represented a state of mind to be personally achieved. Hence it has been remarked that they pursued the knowledge of *tauhid* to dangerous heights, and had to teach their system in secret, employing a special esoteric terminology invented for that purpose (Abdel-Kader, p. 35).

Sufi was just one of many words and titles used in fact, though it is now the most generally applied in the study of the subject, particularly since nineteenth century European scholars created "Sufism." This blanket term, as found in many books on the subject, tends to describe much cult activity as distinct from the more dynamic and evolutionary aspects of the underlying philosophy, which arguably found its representatives in channels not always customarily expected and not easily defined according to armchair convenience.

One of those who underlined the extensions from the conventional Islamic time phase favoured by his culture was Shihabuddin Yahya Sohravardi, known as Al-Maqtul, "the Murdered." The life of this Iranian was prematurely terminated by religious bigots in 1191; his crime in orthodox eyes was heresy, a heresy which included the affirmation that the philosophy of which he was one representative had been a legacy from much earlier times and culture-phases. Not only the Greek philosophers, but also the near extinct Zoroastrian heritage were claimed by Maqtul as precedents in the time chain expressed in abbreviated form in what became known as the *ishraqi* (illuminist) tradition. The *ishraqi* tradition of philosophy distinguished itself over the centuries for its scholarly and scientific capacities, well known in Iran and India; it is less well known, and has even been the cause of puzzlement, that not a few ishraqis neither began nor ended their career as scholars or men of the pen (*ahl-i-qalam*).

Though the complexities of the trends in Shia thought are still largely uncomprehended, it should be evident enough that the theme of the Imamate provided shia thinkers in what Bayat calls "pre-Occultation times" (i.e., prior to the dateline of 873–4 A.D., when the *imam* was pronounced to be alive, ever present in this world, although hidden from ordinary human view) with a doctrinal basis for their tangent from the conventional Sunni majority view. Implicit in the conception of the Imam (leader), explains Bayat, is a belief in a progressive understanding of religion. But tension persisted between progressive and esoteric factions and the conventionally systematized Shia religion which eventually gained ascendancy in Iran. This latter was given codification from the sixteenth century to the nineteenth century by a stratum of high-ranking *ulama* (divines) who were known as *mujtahids.* These high official divines undertook a ruthless campaign against deviation from their doctrinal norms, declaring themselves to be the sole guardians of religous law. Not surprisingly perhaps, their campaign restricted the comparative freedom of thought which had characterized the early formation of Shia Islam; the mujtahids were static in their ruling that further perfecting of Quranic revelation must be postponed until the return of the long-awaited Imam (Bayat, pp. xii–xiii).

Meanwhile, ishraqi philosophers frequently resorted to an obscurantist style of writing, or rather, obscurantist to those who were not well versed in its subtleties of composition. It is apparent that these writers were demanding in the standards set for their audience, and also careful to protect themselves (and their families) from the possible stigma of *takfir,* meaning the accusation of heresy that was wielded by the orthodox divines. (Even in cases where it was not lethal, such stigma could seriously restrict communication prospects and freedom of movement). The ishraqi philosophers practised what was known as *taqiyya,* literally "guarding oneself," a precautionary tactic which they regarded as a necessary virtue and which meant that they concealed their true views from open scrutiny. The reasons are obvious, but as Bayat aptly comments, the social historian may fail to appreciate essential qualities in "Shia theosophy" and reduce it to a mere ideology of intellectual history in attempting to chart the social ramifications of ideas. Henry Corbin, a leading scholar in Iranian studies, repeatedly warned against this tendency, and adamantly stressed the independence of "divine truth" from any social system. (Cf. Bayat, p. xv).

The ishraqis did not constitute a religious sect; their individualistic penchant in general combined diverse interests and accomplishments. Some were themselves members of the *ulama,* but effective, if sophisticated, dissenters. Corbin was the virtual pioneer in the West of deeper aspect studies of this tradition, but arguably concentrated overmuch upon symbolic aspects at the expense of historical and sociocultural intricacies and repercussions.

During the third century after the Islamic invasion of Iran, when it was evident that the Zoroastrian heritage was irreparably waning, a section of the Mazdean priests and others of the Zoroastrian community embarked for India, landing on the coast of Gujarat in the early tenth century. In the greater freedom of India their numbers gradually increased, and they became known as Parsis (Persians).

Those who remained in Iran were very small in number by late medieval times. They were concentrated almost exclusively in the neighbourhoods of Yazd and Kirman. These cities were both set in regions bordered by formidable mountain and desert, and this contributed to an isolation favourable to the maintenance of the old tradition. During the eighteenth century wars decimated the population of Kirman, and the Zoroastrian section of it seems to have become much smaller. But conditions remained unchanged in the Yazd region.

The oasis city of Yazd is situated in Central Iran on a sandy plain notable for fierce summers and very cold winters, a narrow desert tract some thirty miles long that is dotted with numerous villages. It was largely in these rural places, and not in the city, that the Zoroastrian remnant had tenaciously persisted for nearly twelve hundred years by the time of the Qajar dynasty. Life on the Yazd plain was much the same as it had been in the early Middle Ages, even for the Muslim inhabitants. The more far-flung the village, the more exclusively Zoroastrian it was, immaculately preserved from a bygone age.

The adherents of the old faith were largely limited to manual work, being prohibited entry to the trades and professions, since the Muslims wanted no contact with them. Most of them were engaged in agriculture therefore, and their poverty was proverbial. Since open trade was denied them, they maintained a commercial network from their cellars, one that had to be efficient in order to survive. The ban on open trade was not lifted until the mid-nineteenth century, and not until 1882 was the poll-tax (*jizya*) cancelled.

The Zoroastrians were contemptuously referred to as "fire-worshippers," since fire was a sacred symbol to the ancient Persians and still conspicuous in the temples preserved amongst the Yazd community. On their part the Zoroastrians regarded the Muslims as being outside the pale of the true religion. They had maintained a local dialect called Dari which was incomprehensible to users of standard Persian. This dialect was not usually written down, and there were variations from village to village.

This anthropologist's paradise was a continual source of puzzlement and frustration to the more dogmatic Muslims. The situation might be compared to the imaginary analogy of ancient Celtic encampments persisting on Salisbury Plain refusing to acknowledge to the Anglo-Saxon subjects of Queen Victoria that anything had changed since the departure of the Romans from British shores.

The despised gabrs (unbelievers) felt themselves to be the long-suffering victims of the foreign heathen. The city of Yazd was to them the citadel of bigotry, where governors, shia clerics, and tax-collectors occasionally became ogres with regard to the infidel in their midst. It has been said that if a Zoroastrian was murdered, nobody was punished. Converts to Islam were a cause of great rejoicing on the part of the majority, and other Zoroastrian property was sometimes confiscated for the use of the proselytes, regardless of the rightful heirs amongst the maligned community.

In the streets of Yazd, and in any village, it was obligatory for Zoroastrians (Iranis) to walk, and never to ride. Even in the surrounding desert they could only ride donkeys, not horses, and had to dismount upon meeting any Muslim, no matter what rank the latter might be. It was certainly not safe for any Irani to lose patience or control before one of the majority.

Sporadic but vindictive harassments occurred, with mob mood causing forced conversions. This kind of pressure tended to come about if Muslim families moved into a village and gained strength of numbers. Yet there were some villages where members of both religions lived amicably enough, if at arm's length. Muslim converts often retained a basic sympathy for their old faith, and it was these who seem to have acted as a kind of cultural bridge.

The garb of the minority group was retricted to regulation colours, together with the compulsory girdle of rough canvas – the same infidel hallmark that Bayazid Bistami had repeatedly resorted to many centuries earlier.

The Iranist scholar A.V. Williams Jackson visited Yazd in 1903. He reports that while a larger proportion of Zoroastrians outside the city were cultivators, those inside the urban walls were largely occupied in trading, a privilege which they had gained only about fifty years earlier. They had been oppressed by the *jizya* tax until 1882, which had been repealed by Shah Nasr al-Din largely owing to a social influence exerted by the Parsis of Bombay, some of whom had been anxiously at work through the agency of the Society for the Amelioration of the Zoroastrians in Persia, founded in 1854 and which had installed a representative in Iran. It took nearly thirty years to effect the repeal, and prior to 1882, no Zoroastrian was even allowed to build an upper storey on his abode; it was forbidden to erect any dwelling which could extend higher than the upstretched arm of a Muslim. Even within a year after the repeal was issued, a Zoroastrian living in one of the villages is reported to have fled for his life after venturing to add the dignity of an upper room to his house; the troublous episode did not end there, since another Zoroastrian was mistaken for the culprit and killed by the enraged Muslims. Even now, wrote Jackson in 1903, the beleaguered community were not permitted to ride in the streets, and they were still subject to many petty annoyances. Only recently, in 1898, Shah Muzaffar al-Din had issued a further decree seeking to alleviate Zoroastrian grievances; this decree was imperfectly observed, adds our witness.

According to Jackson, the number of Zoroastrians in Yazd had increased over the last half-century from 6,658 in 1854 to between 8,000 and 8,500 in 1903. He attributes this rise in population to a lesser degree of intolerance, aided by the restraining presence of Europeans and possibly also by the spread of Babist (or neo-Babist) doctrines which favoured religious liberty. Yet it seems doubtful as to whether this latter factor counted very much, for the Babi sect was the victim of a sporadic persecution that was often savage. Even while Jackson was in Yazd, there was a general Muslim rising against the Babis, a large number of whom were concentrated in Yazd. Hundreds of these people, who habitually pleaded for toleration, were massacred by their countrymen or subjected to what Jackson describes as shocking outrages. Had it not been for the prudent intervention of Europeans on this occasion, the persecution might easily have extended to hapless Zoroastrians.

A report of an earlier visit to Yazd by a reliable witness gives that much more of a grim picture of life for the oppressed minority. The orientalist scholar E.G. Browne appeared on the scene in 1887–8, and while he was in Yazd, a Zoroastrian was bastinadoed for *accidentally* touching with his garment some fruit that was for sale in the bazaar, an infidel action that was considered to render the fruit unclean for consumption by true believers.

It may take an effort for the reader to imagine what conditions may have been like before the 1882 repeal.

Browne relates that only about twelve years prior to his visit (that is, *circa* 1875), the Muslims had threatened to sack the Zoroastrian quarter and kill all gabrs who would not embrace Islam; this was in retaliation for a Muslim having been killed by a Zoroastrian, according to the allegation. The unrest subsided after a Muslim was legally executed for the murder of a Zoroastrian woman. One hopes that the woman's death was not too violent.

Earlier, the annals of Yazd were particularly bloodstained during the period of unrest following the death of Muhammad Shah in 1848 and prior to the accession of the new Qajar monarch Nasiruddin Shah. Many Zoroastrians, relates Browne, were at that time robbed, beaten, and threatened with death unless they became converts to Islam. A large number were killed, and Browne met one old Zoroastrian who had been the victim of several pistol shots from the oppressors, as penalty for his refusal to change religion. The difference between life and death must have been slender.

Browne estimated the number of Zoroastrians in the

Yazd area at between seven to ten thousand, and says that from his own experience of them (both at Yazd and distant Kirman), he formed a very high opinion of their honesty, integrity and industry. He was clearly impressed by their "decorous conduct," and also comments upon their physical features; their religous tradition had prevented their intermarriage with Arabs, Turks, and other non-Aryan breeds, and hence the Zoroastrians represented the purest Iranian stock, whose physical beauty was striking.

Much of the savage brutality directed at the persecuted minority appears to have come from the local roughnecks known as *lutis* (exactly how much manipulation was brought to bear from other Islamic factions is a relevant question however). Yet even the *lutis* had their complexities; there were better and worse elements amongst them. The best of this trend constituted, according to Floor, a popular movement harbouring ideals of social justice, equality, and even high morals. The social ideas of such *lutis,* or *lutigars,* inevitably involved them in political matters, but at the point of aggression, many of them merged into an unfortunate liaison with criminal groups and tendencies. This happened in all the major cities like Yazd and Isfahan; the *lutis* were very much an urban phenomenon in Qajar Iran, amounting to local sporting clubs which distinguished themselves from the rest of society by unorthodox garb which must have struck an acute note of terror in the psychological associations of Zoroastrians. At their worst, the *lutis* were a criminal class by Floor's definition; they would attack and rob peacable citizens, and contrary to Islamic law, they would drink alcohol and commit adultery. Yet the Shah of Persia did not refrain from making use of these delinquents; they provided a ready source of manpower, and by their participation in power politics provided an extra income to the patron prepared to receive part of the profit accruing from their criminal activities.

Strong arm hooliganism in Qajar Iran must have been facilitated by the gymnastic activities of many *lutis*. This extended at one extreme to duels frequently being fought between individual *lutis* or between group leaders, with no quarter being given nor asked. Though such intercenine aggression was popular amongst them, they would act in concert against outsiders. It was reported in the 1850's by a European traveller that the *lutigar* hostility towards outsiders was aided by affiliation with the Haidari and Nimati (Nimatullahi) dervish orders. That dervish orders could become fanatical is no surprise to any historian of the subject, but it has to be remembered that such affiliation could also have been at least part of the cause for the more idealistic strains among the *lutis*.

The fact remains that a mob of *lutis* spurred on by a *Quran*-punching *mulla* (religious scholar) or the local governor must have required a certain tenacity of endurance on the part of the oppressed minority of non-Muslims. A few Zoroastrians seem to have left their homes and hereditary holdings to seek a rugged shelter in the mountains surrounding the Yazd plain. They were prohibited from leaving the country, but the more adventurous managed to do so in secret. There seems to have been only a trickle of such departures however, since most preferred to endure the indignities and keep what they had rather than face the extreme uncertainties of change. India was the main objective of the emigrants, but the more prosperous Parsi community in India did not begin to make any firm contact with the Yazd counterpart until the mid-nineteenth century. By the time that this communication was effectively furthered, it was too late in date to concern our immediate subject.

The main reason why most of the Irani Zoroastrians were unventuresome was the acute environmental isolation and accompanying ignorance of the outside world. The Yazd plain was to all practical purposes an island, and a non-existent port of call if you were a Zoroastrian. The only regular Islamic visitors were in the shape of camel caravans. It was over a week's laborious journey to the nearest cities, namely Kirman, Isfahan, and Shiraz. It could take as long as three weeks to reach Tehran, the Qajar capital to the north, where there were only fifty Zoroastrians in 1854. The roads were dangerous owing to numerous brigands who were quite capable of murder, and lethal sandstorms which could seriously damage sight and hearing. The drifting sands and mountain terrain walled in the Zoroastrians of the Yazd locale. This plain was their world; what dread uncertainties lay beyond it?

One of the villages on this plain was Khooramshah, its origins pre-dating the Islamic invasion in the seventh century, at which time the town was walled in an attempt at fortification. This measure did not stop the Arabs, who afterwards left the inhabitants alone after giving them the alternative to accept Islam or pay the poll-tax. The high turreted walls continued to shelter Zoroastrians, whose civic life underwent drastic changes, but whose religious ways continued as before.

When Sheriar Mundegar Irani was born here in 1853, the gaunt walls still stood, the narrow lanes were still peopled by the worshippers of Ahuramazda. He was brought up in the common poverty, though his father Mundegar was not an agricultural worker. Instead the latter drew a pittance from his employment as keeper (*salar*) of the tower of silence (*dakhma*) a few miles away.

Such towers are burial places of a unique type, set well apart from human habitation. Zoroastrianism affirmed the sacred qualities of fire and earth, and this led to the orthodox prohibition of both cremation and burial. Special towers open to the sky were therefore constructed, and corpses placed inside for vultures to clean the bones, which were removed at intervals for special interment. The guardians of such towers, together with the corpse-bearers (*khandias*), were regarded with respect by the rest of Zoroastrian society, but had to adhere to a special set of taboos, since they were considered to be contaminated. They led a strict life in conformity with ritualistic purity, and were obliged to lead a semi-segregated existence even amongst their own families.

When Sheriar was only five years old, his mother died. There was nobody to look after him at home, and so he began to accompany his father to the tower of silence. He would remain with him all day long, helping his father in his duties, talking with him in lieu of an education, joining him in prayer, and observing the ancient rites.

The site of this tower was known as Kasimabad, a deserted and solitary location after the traditional pattern.

Upon a gaunt hill overlooking the sandy wastes was a large, squat circular tower, completely open to the sky. It is not surprising that this structure showed signs of advanced decay, since it was centuries old; it was probably a replacement of an earlier structure in which Sassanian corpses were deposited. (There are now two other towers alongside the dilapidated original; one seems to have been constructed about the mid-nineteenth century, and the other is modern). At the foot of this hill where time had effectively stood still, were a range of buildings which included brick urns used for the attendant custom of baking bread by the relatives of the deceased. Mundegar Irani's main duty was to mark out a consecrated line with a stick around any corpse that was brought to him, and read out prayers from the *Zend-Avesta* as a sanction for the corpse-bearers to carry the body up to the platform inside the tower for consequent disposal.

Young Sheriar became accustomed to the intense solitude of Kasimabad, since his father sometimes left him in charge for several hours. One day when he was barely seven years old, he was left on his own while his father went into town that morning on a business errand. Mundegar intended to return in the afternoon, but was unable to do so as it transpired. While twilight descended, the corpse of a child was brought into the compound of the tower in readiness for the final rites. In the absence of the keeper, the body was left outside the tower by the corpse-bearers, after which they departed. Twilight deepended into darkness, but still Mundegar did not return. A silence prevailed in the bleak precincts, occasionally broken by the shrill scream of vultures. The site was a reputedly eerie spot in the darkness, regarded with the circumspect awe which often clings to places of the dead. The night was pitch-black, and the boy had no lamp. Yet he remained at his post with the corpse as his sole human companion, expecting his father's return at any moment. He felt that he should guard the corpse against the vultures on behalf of his parent, since the body had yet to be prepared for the tower in the customary manner. When at length he began to feel sleepy, he conceived the idea of tying the corpse to his foot with a piece of string in order to prevent the ravenous vultures from dragging away their accustomed prey. The watcher fell asleep before his father returned.

Childhood was a stark experience for Sheriar Irani. His father was poor, he had no mother, his community was an oppressed minority group. He and his kind had to keep a constantly vigilant eye upon potential Muslim troublemakers. He grew up on stories, or rather facts, of theft, arson and rape committed by the brutish element amongst the opposing community. The towers of silence were liable to be desecrated, raids were occasionally made on fire temples to snuff out the sacred flame. Gangs of youths might bully someone if they got the opportunity, jibing that the gabrs must be wrong in their beliefs since there were far fewer of them than Muslims. These delinquent forms of behaviour and logic occur too often in modern cities to be considered a particular failing of religion.

Sheriar would later relate a graphic anecdote concerning the daily round of the Zoroastrian males. They would keep a pole embedded in the ground at the entrance to their homes. Before going out to work in the mornings, they would assault these poles with what amounted to a fit of violence: kicking, spitting, and even showering abuse upon these inanimate objects. These poles represented Muslim aggressors, and supplied an outlet for retaliation feelings which placed them in danger if expressed in any other manner. However, they did sometimes even the score a little; Sheriar knew a man who threw an insolent Muslim youth down a well-shaft when no other Muslim was in sight.

In the presence of death, of carrion flesh and bleached bones, he gained a degree of insulation from loneliness, fear, the threat of oppression. Silence did not hold for him the terrors that it does for some moderns. He knew how everyone was going to end up in the everyday world; all his community would one day come to Kasimabad in the hands of the corpse-bearers. Even the Muslims would die. This did not produce in him any shallow "live while you can" philosophy; the long hours of vigil contributed to a contemplative capacity to detach from his environment. He realized that he was beginning to see things differently from others, that they were limited by immediate horizons which they could not evaluate in a manner other than the most crudely obvious.

He found himself estranged from others of his age. This was partly because of his continual presence at the tower, by virtue of which he participated in the *salar* contamination which society deemed best to avoid. Other boys tended to shrink from him, and this caused him to closely analyze human reactions. He found himself unmoved by the trinkets and simple pleasures which constituted their apogee of contentment. He was becoming a stranger to both communities on the Yazd plain.

He gained no schooling in the usual sense of the word, and remained illiterate. Yet he was steeped in the oral tradition of the old texts, appropriating from his father the doctrines which had been maintained on the desolate, sand-swept hill of Kasimabad since the Sassanian era. This was not all however. There were oral traditions amongst the Muslims which seeped through the religious barriers, albeit garbled perhaps, but which were tantalizing to one who became receptive to them. This folklore, if one can call it such, appeared to indicate something more than worship, something more than ritual. He heard of strange lands and peoples, and may well have seen dervishes pass by on their itineraries.

Every day he looked out from his hill-top to the lofty mountains across the sands. What lay beyond those mountains? Everyone was scared of entering them, apprehensive of known and unknown dangers. His father could not satisfy him on this point. He began to feel a stranger in Khooramshah, while the tower of silence seemed to have taught him all it could.

He began to see his community situation in the light of an automatic pattern of constrictions imposed by birth and environment. In effect, he began to starkly view the cultural milieu shorn of the insistent network of associations which cloud the brain's capacity to assess in larger terms.

Orthodox religion could not satisfy his need, which had become too great. He wanted a greater liberty, a greater equality, and a greater fraternity than he had formerly known.

One day Sheriar Irani walked away from the grim tower of silence, going down the hill and into the sandy wastes towards the mountains. He knew that there were no guarantees of survival. He boldly departed into the unknown, never to return.

He was only thirteen years old.

From the later reminiscences of the wanderer, three basic developments are clearly discernible:

(a) The first four years were extremely difficult, entailing much hardship and requiring great determination to continue. There is little doubt that by the time he was sixteen, he was mature in the art of self-preservation.

(b) He travelled widely throughout Iran, and his later references were strewn with tales of deserts, mountains, and long treks on foot. These stories became largely amorphous in the minds of his listeners who were unacquainted with the terrain and way of life he spoke of, and who were unfamiliar with the attitude of mind underlying the anecdotes. Owing to this, there is very little in the way of explicit geographical references available.

(c) He contacted fairly large numbers of persons known as dervishes and sufis. The Persian word *dervish* commonly signified one who begged in the mendicant manner, though the degree of mendicancy differed. The tag of dervish was very frequently synonymous with *sufi*, a generalization which did not contribute to the quality of usage of the latter term.

Sheriar encountered frequent criticism and ridicule from Muslims, since it took him some time to adjust to the different cultural atmosphere through which he now passed. His main problem was food, but not everybody wanted to give sustenance to a fire-worshipping mendicant. If he did not get food, whether from nature or from kitchens, he simply had to go hungry. But he was inured to poverty, and accustomed to being wary of potential enemies.

Though by virtue of his religious background and underdog social experiences Sheriar was at loggerheads with Islam, he was able to align himself with the more liberal forms of sufi affiliation. The saga of Al-Hallaj fired young

Sheriar in a way that will be readily understandable even to the more hardened critics of Persian Sufism. When your compatriots are raped and beaten by the mob, you will inevitably admire someone who reportedly had his tongue cut out for telling the truth at civic level.

The environmental background in which Sheriar Irani was able to equate himself with the more liberal Sufism is not well known nor accurately represented in the majority of works readily accessible to the public in the "mystical" field. Sufism at large was not glamorous or homogenous, but a hybrid which included forms of fanaticism and degeneracy that were not unique to Qajar Iran. Yet it was often the only vehicle of protest against state anomalies. Popular dervish movements in Iran were sporadically in danger of severe persecution from the imperial and theological authorities; the fate of dervish leaders had often been lethally precarious under totalitarian rule in the Safavid and post-Safavid eras. Yet it was not only the ecclesiastical and political authorities who displayed defects from the viewpoint of a Zoroastrian observer.

It is possible that the movement now known as Babism played a substantial part in accommodating young Sheriar Irani to sufi trends. Babism was one of the Iranian phenomena that fascinated E.G. Browne, who wrote of these socioreligious revolutionaries with sympathy. More recently, Kazeni has pertinently commented on the different social ingredients of the Babi movement: some Western historians have suggested that Babism was in effect a bourgeois movement addressed to merchants and the middle classes, though Kazeni stresses that the number of merchants among early converts appears to have been smaller than the number of Shia religious leaders who were attracted to the movement. This attraction becomes more notable when it is realized that the founder of the movement strongly attacked the corruption amongst the religious divines. As Kazeni aptly remarks, there was no room for the clergy in the founder's system, which at least partially explains the violent reactions of those clergy who did not become Babis. It seems true enough that the Shi'ite clergy were displeased with the expansion of the Western powers and the ineptness of the central government of Iran. The increasing tyranny of the Qajar government may well have contributed to the incentive of those clergy who became Babi converts. It may be even more significant however that there was strong support for the Babi movement in rural areas of Isfahan, Mazandaran, and Azarbaijan. The peasants and lower classes were confronted with a general deterioration of their socioeconomic position; the policy of the central government was not in the interests of the population at large, giving rise to the complaint of rising taxes which were substantially exacted in order to prepare an army for military engagements with the Russians. The messianic overtones of Babism must indeed have met with eager reception amongst many low class people, and no wonder perhaps in view of their plight.

The actual messianic content of Babism has not escaped argument. Kazeni remarks that Mirza Ali Muhammad's claim to be the Bab ("Gate") was ambiguous in relation to both Shia and Shaikhi doctrines (the latter being a very recent addition to Iranian mystico-religious formulations). The designation of *Bab* is etymologically traceable to early Shi'ism, in which era it was used to refer to the senior disciples of the Imam. It was consequently not at first clear as to whether Mirza Ali Muhammad was referring to himself as the "gate" to the hidden imam of Shia lore, or that he deemed himself to be the awaited Imam. Some historians support the former perspective, though Kazeni stresses that the Bab soon made known that he was the awaited *mahdi,* an assertion made public before the hostile *ulama* of Tabriz during the government tribunal in 1847–8.

It is perhaps interesting to speculate upon what version of all this percolated to Sheriar Irani. Even if he understood the issue of mahdism somewhat differently to Shia theologians, he may well have concluded that the religious liberty advocated by latter day Babis was decidedly preferable to less tolerant prospects. The fact is that Babis (at least after 1860) were sympathetic to Zoroastrians; Sheriar's contact with the movement would have registered the Bahai overtones which adopted a pacifist outlook from the 1860's onwards, in contrast with the earlier militancy of the movement. (The Bahai sect was an offshoot from Babism, and was pacifist from its inception).

The government tribunal at Tabriz perhaps merits further clarification in terms of social trends. The subject of victimization was Mirza Ali Muhammad, born at Shiraz in 1820. This son of a cloth-merchant was known for his austere ways, early abandoning commercial pursuits and gaining the respect of many learned Muslims and also the enmity of the less partial Shi'ite divines. Browne says that Ali Muhammad gained a conviction that he was the reformer and saviour of his nation. He proclaimed himself as the Bab in 1844. Rumours began to circulate that the Imam Mahdi had come at last to establish universal justice and peace. But the government became alarmed at the rapid growth of the movement, and accordingly issued orders for the Bab to be confined in Shiraz. Retribution was harsh: some Babis were beaten and mutilated, and all the Bab's followers were prohibited from discussing his doctrines in public. There was a strong resentment, and his followers continued to propagate his doctrines (and quite conceivably their own also) while the Bab himself was transported to and fro in imprisonment. There was an extremely determined opposition from the orthodox party, headed by leading ecclesiastical divines. It is true to say that the opposing factions were daggers drawn, for they came into armed collision upon the death of the monarch Muhammad Shah in 1848. There were substantial insurrections of Babis at Yazd, Niriz, Zanjan and Mazandaran, involving savage conflicts with the royalist forces. Browne emphasized that the Bab was innocent of any direct participation in the plans or councils of the rebels. This made no difference to the government however; since Mirza Ali Muhammad was now regarded as the figurehead of the whole anti-authority enterprise, it was officially decided to execute him. Orders were despatched to Tabriz to bring him out from prison, give him a formal trial, and then terminate his existence. Browne's account says of the Bab's end in 1850 that he was dragged through the streets for many hours, though he maintained the composure which had characterized the whole duration of his imprisonment. A large crowd witnessed this finale, including those who were sympathetic and others who were vindictive towards the arch-heretic. The execution was by shooting, but the first volley merely cut the ropes suspending him in mid-air. He fell to the ground unhurt, and the panic-stricken shooting squad refused to fire again. Superstitious awe or call it what you will, the squad had to be replaced in order for governmental decisions to be carried out. This time, the body of the young Shiraz heretic was effectively riddled with bullets. His corpse was demonstratively dragged through the streets and contemptuously cast out beyond the city gates to be devoured by jackals and dogs.

There were later schisms in the Babi movement, and a great deal more persecution from the authorities.

If it is true, as Bayat concludes, that the Bab did incite to militant revolt, then his example is not dissimilar to some Marxist emphases. It would have been very difficult for a non-literate person like Sheriar to determine exactly what the Bab's standpoint had been. Bahai sources portray the Bab and his chief disciples as peace-loving people, but the tone of Babi letters during the late 1840's reveals an opposite tendency (Bayat, p. 96). Though the Bab did counsel his followers to avoid violence and make converts peaceably, he also explicitly condoned coercive measures and holy war for the purpose of forcing unbelievers to follow the right path (Bayat, p. 106).

Babism did not remain a separate watertight compartment from other aspects of Iranian sociocultural life. As described by Browne, for instance, there was evidently a strange mixture of persecuted Babism and the category of dervish known as *qalandar*. These *qalandars* had a reputation for unorthodoxy and varied somewhat in disposition and affiliation, but many of them were no more than loquacious drunkards and opium-addicts. In his chapter on the *qalandars* in his travel narrative, Browne describes (pp. 572–3) a dervish of the Nimatullahi order who smoked a great quantity of opium and was also in the habit of reciting much mystical poetry. It was a favourite ploy of these aberrant *qalandar* types to exclaim: "I am Moses! I am Jesus! I am Muhammad!" Apart from the more exhibitionist features of such idioms, they can at least partly be viewed in the context of popular trends opposing authority figures. These idioms had for long been a stock feature of popular Iranian Sufism, and probably originated with more dynamic entities such as Bayazid Bistami and Hallaj. Hallaj possessed a very dexterous mind, as is evident from his writings alone, and he cannot fairly be equated with such as Shah Ismail (d.1524), the ruthless founder of the Safavid dynasty who was capable of writing heretical poetry in which he gained divine status.

Since some Babis were dervishes, it is the more pertinent to stress that young Sheriar Irani's fear of persecution would have continued even in a neo-Babi guise. The lethal penalties meted out to Babi rebels by the government authorities and gloating *mujtahids* were grim enough even by Zoroastrian standards – persecutors would customarily ram fatal wads of cloth down the throats of Babi victims with the aid of mallets (details abbreviated for the sake of the squeamish). It is doubtful whether our Zoroastrian dervish ever dared to voice qalandari axioms even in the solitary wilderness.

Though I have been unable to verify what connections Sheriar may or may not have had with the Babis, I have been able to ascertain his dilemma with regard to popular Sufism and pious Islamic "sufis".

Barring the *mujtahids,* a greater source of trouble to him than the everyday mentality Muslims were the professed sufis whom he encountered. He found that some of these exhibited the traits of (to put it mildly) vain and malicious hypocrites. To his dismay he found that the dervish orders were anything but exempt from the formalists who crept into the ranks to bask in the limelight that frequently accrued to them in the public eye, the false credentials of their venerable appearance being taken at surface value by the ignorant. Their attitude towards the young wanderer was censorious time and again. It was not only that they saw him to be a gabr, but the fact that he was youthful and had no status comparable to their own provoked manifestations of the superiority complex from the assertive elect. It no doubt took him a little while before he learnt how to deal with such proud imposters.

With typical humour he would later tell of how he arrived

one day at the town of Baft Badanjan (this was probably the rural town of Baft in the Kirman region). Being hungry, he approached a baker and asked for alms in the accepted mendicant manner. When the baker was about to give him a loaf of bread, a local dervish appeared upon the scene requesting the daily portion that he usually received from the baker's shop. But the baker declined to oblige him, informing him that his accustomed share would go that day to his young brother dervish. The local ascetic was angered at what he took to be an incursion upon his patronage, and began to arrogantly remonstrate with the baker. "Why should you feed him at my expense?" was the burden of his refrain. The baker replied (approximately): "You take bread from here every day; why should you grumble if for once I give your share to this dervish, who is so young and in need?" The local holy man was accustomed to gaining his own way; he threw a contemptuous glance at the gabr and said to his patron scathingly: "How dare you call such an urchin a dervish! I challenge him to answer my questions if he really thinks that he is a dervish!"

By this time a number of onlookers had gathered round, mostly curious loiterers who miss nothing that savours of dissension. With the expectation of extracting entertainment from the contest, they requested Sheriar to take up the challenge. The baker also urged him to accept, having become indignant at the attitude of the local. Sheriar was at first reluctant to enter into a dialectical contest, being reserved by nature and indisposed to such wrangles. This was probably not merely because of his lack of schooling, but because he was wary of incurring hostility. He did not want to be beaten up by the local *lutis,* who could leave even a Goliath much worse than they found him; nor can he have wanted to risk a potentially lethal harangue from any fanatical *mulla* owing to his ignorance of the *Quran*. After some reflection however, he decided that it was best to accede to the wishes of those present. There followed a lively controversy which from the beginning went against the arrogant dervish, and the bystanders soon grasped that the young Zoroastrian knew more and argued more ably than his bombastic opponent. Finally the complacent senior found that he was losing face, which prompted him to beat a hasty retreat amidst the jeers of the spectators. Sheriar was then congratulated by the crowd, and given a loaf of bread by the baker as his reward.

Our traveller became accustomed to the fact that not all so-called sufis are worthy of respect; he concluded that real teachers are extremely rare. He saw instead the imposters who duped the public, the ingenious actors, the rogues, the profligates, the sincere but sadly deluded leaders, the well-meaning pedants who were lost without a book in front of them. His introduction to the subject was hard, but it taught him how to evaluate the "mystical." He was in effect what has sometimes been termed an *uwaysi,* one who follows sufi modes of discipline and thought without joining any dervish order; the term derives from the seventh century Arab mystic Uways al-Qarni, a contemporary of Muhammad who did not join the early Islamic community. The *uwaysi* may be at a disadvantage without a teacher, but he is better off without one than with the wrong one. Traditional lore has it that a very serious error is to develop pride in imagined accomplishments, and to think that no teacher is necessary.

While taking his cue from the oral tradition, and journeying in search of clues to contemporary sages, Sheriar learnt a great deal about his country and its people. He saw above his childhood hatred of the Muslims for their oppression; the plight of many poor Muslims deeply moved him. He was amazed at the ruins of past cultures which he encountered along his routes. Even many of the inhabited towns and cities through which he passed were largely crumbling and deserted, acute testimony to the wars of the previous century and the economic problem current in Qajar times. Above all, he saw how everyone was the constrained psychological product of their livelihood and information background – how they tended to focus upon only a fragment of life insofar as it directly concerned their daily round, effectively blind to the extensive trail of implications which lead from this. The perception was nurtured in our traveller at contemplative levels, and perpetually goaded him onwards with fresh strength to find an ultimate meaning. He knew that he had been severely limited to only one set of cultural associations during his childhood, a cordon which the tower of silence had given him the means to break. How much more could he break through the associational net imposed by the mind, normally information-doped, but which clearly had increasingly finer boundaries to be recognized, finer boundaries composed of increasingly larger units of reference. This does not mean to say that his life programme is to be measured in terms of a mere quantity of experience; rather, the crucial factor would appear to be that of a specially absorbed quality of experience. Unless one lives for centuries, that is the only logical hope of a worthwhile definition occurring in consciousness.

He willingly passed through the solitudes of vast desert wastes and mountain fastnesses where awesome silence reigned, a silence which might produce madness in the over-civilized, but which gave him a deep peace regardless of the accompanying privations. He learnt how even in the desert one can live, finding solace in grim nature after the oppression and confusion of human society. He often slept in the open with rocks or trees as his only shelter. But always he would return sooner or later to the beaten tracks of civilization, passing through the towns and villages to complement his emerging focus of awareness. As he grew older, spectators were not aware so much that he was a Zoroastrian. He was just another dust-strewn dervish, speaking a few words in straightforward Persian. He knew too well how people reacted if they thought you were different; it worried them, irritated them, posed a threat to their horizons, set their attention upon you to an unwarranted degree. The best thing to do was to blend in as unobtrusively as possible, even though he knew only a few words of the *Quran*. That way he was more likely to find out where gangs of *lutis* were concentrated, and who was likely to commit the next murder. Life was tough on the road in Qajar Iran, whether in urban or rural locations; some dervishes would carry knives or even axes, and the latter accoutrement was arguably not always intended as a purely symbolic appendage, but as a means of defence.

A significant section of the population of Iran were

nomadic, then far more so than now. Some tribal groups like the Qashqai and Afshars are of Turkish stock, others like the Kurds and Luris are thought to possess very ancient Indo-European blood. The brigand element amongst the tribes were feared for their robberies, and it was said that they would kill you if they thought you were a coward or an interferer. Yet in the tents could often be found a warm hospitality that was practically a code of honour. Our traveller must have encountered some of the tribes, and even the brigands might conceivably have warmed towards a plucky young mendicant with bitter memories of city-dwellers. In the nomadic view, man had too much neglected the old ways for too long. He had altogether lost the migratory rhythm between summer and winter. City men tried to shut themselves in from nature, thought they could do everything better than nature did it. What kind of consequences would this perversity produce? Their women were stronger than city men. The so-called civilized inhabitants tried to impose order upon what they thought was chaos, and produced the most elaborate chaos in the process, with wars and mass suffering in accompaniment that were worse than any tribal feud. City men tried to make everything neat and straight, and robbed things of their natural qualities by forcing them into pigeonholes. It was the tribal affirmation that only *Allah* can achieve perfect order.

Sheriar Irani was undeniably an adherent of the natural life, living as close to nature as it is physically possible to do so. He even made it a firm rule never to accept money from anybody, only begging for food when he was hungry. But he knew that neither the natural life nor the cultured city existence are helpful if they become an end in themselves without an inner regeneration to avoid distortions. The daggers of tribal bandits drew blood as red as the assaults of the *lutis* were notorious for. In the north-east of Iran, the villages were subject to raids from Turkoman tribesmen who would emerge from the Turkestan frontier in pursuit of human cargo to be sold into slavery in non-Iranian territory. At best the victims were held for ransom, at worst they were killed en route if they proved unduly burdensome.

Sheriar evidently learnt that there was safety in numbers sometimes, since he later referred to other dervish comrades. I have not been able to ascertain their identity; it is my supposition that they were Babist types, defiant *qalandars,* or the more moderate Nimatullahis who risked persecution at times of civic friction. He may not have deemed them all to be equally savoury or dedicated, but such acquaintances would have provided him with a certain amount of protection, and also provided him with a communications factor relating to the Qajar version of news bulletins. He might have learnt where the army was stationed, how many jewels the Shah of Iran had studded in his throne and scabbard, how many peasants were thought to have gone hungry in last year's drought, how many inches of beard the local *mujtahid* could boast to prove his sagacious sanctity while dining on the best food provided by the peasantry.

There were also more positive elements that may have circulated via the dervish oral grapevine. It is not impossible that he may have heard of Haji Mulla Sabzavari (d.1878) of Khorasan, who is likely to have received favourable reports among dervish groupings. Iranian scholars inevitably refer to him with a partisan zeal, but when the Soviet scholar Bertels could approvingly state that Sabzavari was in no sense an imitator of the classical philosophers, one realizes that favourable reports are not unfounded. Browne called Sabzavari the greatest philosopher of nineteenth century Iran; he was heir to the *ishraqi* heritage passing through Amili, Findiriski and Mulla Sadra Shirazi, whose written teachings he used as his means of communication, since the *ishraqi* heritage had become acceptable to the Shia divines in its modified form. Sabzavari was noted for his kindness, sympathy and liberality to the poor of all descriptions, while despising contact with the aristocrats and wary of the rich clergy.

Nasr writes that Sabzavari led an extremely simple life that resembled more the sufi penchant than the ways of a learned *hakim.* It is said that in addition to his regular students whom he instructed in his *madrasa* at his native Sabzavar, he also taught sufi lore to special pupils. Certainly, he had plenty of candidates to choose from: students from diverse areas of Iran, India, and the Arab countries came to this distant town in Khorasan, a town of distinctly rural standards by comparison with Mashhad. One of these pupils was Sultan Ali Shah Gunabad, alias Haji Mulla Sultan, who provided the incentive for the Gunabadi "order," regarded as an offshoot of the Nimatullahi dervish order. The Gunabadis were strikingly non-bourgeois in their composition, and came to include many working-class people in Iran.

Rypka has notably stated that the philosophy of Sabzavari merits the serious attention of Western thinkers. Browne (who was far from being uncritical) commented that he deemed this philosophy remarkable, and added that his fieldwork tended to contradict the ideas formed by most European scholars of the philosophy current in Iran. In this connection, he made an interesting observation on the possible extent to which the concealment of opinions prevailed in Iran, a strategy rendered necessary owing to the power and rabid intolerance of the clergy, since many philosophers and sufis had forfeited their lives in expressing their views freely and openly.

It is intriguing to consider what reception an unlettered Zoroastrian dervish might have received at Sabzavari's abode. One does not doubt but that he would have at least received a loaf of bread, and very possibly some sage advice. Such a mendicant would not however have stood much chance of enrolling in one of the classes, since Sabzavari's formal curriculum demanded a high degree of literacy and a satisfactory knowledge of preliminary studies even before starting.

With regard to the atmosphere of concealed opinion, it seems that this lodged with Sheriar Irani into much later periods of his life; he appears to me to have been the epitome of reticence with regard to matters that everybody else might not have understood. This aspect of his psychology is the more easily understandable when it is realized that even the more hot-headed and socially demonstrative Babis inclined to aggression were like clams by the 1880's as proven by the travels of Browne. How could they not be so secretive when the penalty was diabolical torture instigated by the pious and self-seeking *mujtahids*?

Sheriar is known to have acquired some knowledge of the dubious subject of astrology during his dervishi; significantly perhaps, he did not stress the subject in his later years, and very little is known of his precise attitude towards it. Of possible relevance here is Browne's acquaintance with a pupil of Sabzavari who accepted that there was an intrinsic validity in astrology, though viewing most of those who flaunted it as mere imposters. These philosophers held that the subject required very long study before its real context was learnt, by which time one understood it to mean something completely different from what was in circulation amongst gullible fools.

Though Sheriar never returned to Khooramshah, the inhabitants there eventually heard that the departee had become a dervish who travelled around the country. Because their information on the departee was hopelessly scanty, the only tag which some could apply to him as a description of his vocation was that of "singing the *sama*." *Sama* literally means "hearing" or audition, and is commonly applied to dervish music and song, though it does not necessarily apply to music at all, but to recitation of the *Quran*. I have no doubt that our subject may well have warbled a few, or even several, dervish ditties, if only to seem like one of the gang.

Sama may well have been an ingredient of dervish pilgrimages he may have joined to places like Mahan or Shiraz. In fairness to dervishes, they often took such proceedings far more seriously than the modern tourist attitude of going to a place simply in order to say that one has been there.

One of the cities he is most likely to have visited is Shiraz, set in a picturesque mountain valley in south-west Iran. Only thirty miles from Shiraz are the ruins of Persepolis, the royal palace of the Persian empire which met its end some fifteen hundred years before the birth of the famous poet Saadi, himself a dervish of some sort in the thirteenth century. Though an evocative ruin, Persepolis is less likely to have been the focus of Sheriar's attention than the tombs of Saadi or Hafiz, apart from Babi and other associations. Hafizian verses were well known amongst dervishes, in general regarded as symbolic, though not a few *qalandars* were facile enough in interpreting them literally. Some of these individuals required little excuse to imbibe the less allegorical wine in generous quantities; there is every indication however that Sheriar felt deeply offended by this habit. It must have been as difficult to obtain accurate information from a drunken *qalandar* as from a cold sober but fanatical *mujtahid*.

There have been diverse scholastic deliberations over what the *Diwan* of Hafiz is supposed to comprise in terms of authentic verses, let alone the actual meaning of the contents. Sheriar Irani made a close study of the *Diwan* in the version available to him in his later years, and did let fall indications that he found more within its pages than mere poetic appeal. He may not have been quite so influenced by standardized sufistic interpretations as might at first appear; for instance, even in his earlier years, Sheriar must have wondered exactly what was meant by the Hafizian designation of "magian," a term of more than passing interest to an infidel fire-worshipper. The Hafizian poems refer to the "*pir* of the magians" (*pir-i-mughan*), and he might justifiably have pondered as to whether this *pir* (old man, sage) was really of the same category as the *pirs* and *murshids* of popular Sufism, regardless of Shia extrapolations from a more Sunnized epoch that in turn had elements in common with earlier forms of Shi'ism.

It may here be appropriate to refer to the report concerning Ahmed al-Ghazali (d.1126), whose fame was largely eclipsed and obscured by that of his brother Abu Hamid who gained the sobriquet of the "Proof of Islam." Al-Murtada has it that the wandering dervish Ahmed arrived in Baghdad and accused his brother, then theological professor of the Nizamiyya Academy, of having taken the role of teacher and preacher but neglecting to be taught.

When Sheriar Irani encountered his brother Khododad once again, it was not perhaps comparable to the encounter of the Ghazali brothers, but did contribute to a change in the pattern of his dervishi. I have not been able to ascertain the location of their meeting, but it is reported that Sheriar did not return to Khooramshah (it may have been at Tehran, amongst the newly emerging Zoroastrian community in the capital). Sheriar found that his brother was keen to emigrate to India, but was appalled at his materialistic horizons. He could well understand why Khododad wanted to escape the hereditary poverty, but he was sorry to see this compulsion obliterate any concept of a finer aim. Khododad on his part could not understand what motivated his dervish brother, thinking exclusively in terms of amassing money, something for which he showed an inherent flair.

The reasons for Sheriar's decision to depart from Iran are not difficult to fathom. As an underdog in the Qajar environment, even in dervish guise, he was understandably attracted to the prospect of different conditions in which persecution was absent. There was by now a concrete knowledge of Bombay amongst Irani Zoroastrians.

Sheriar had been a mendicant for about eight years. Amongst the lessons he had learnt was that the concept of a "sufi" varied according to different types of mentality, and that it is usually the bogus who offers all the standard adjuncts of the commonly desired ideal, something in the manner of a tailor-made straitjacket.

The upshot was that the brothers Sheriar and Khododad agreed to combine their initiative upon a voyage to British India. It was *circa* 1874 when they made a tedious crossing to Bombay.

The city of Bombay on the west coast of the Indian peninsula was even then a teeming metropolis of Asiatic humanity, dominated by the British overlords who had created their Indian empire half a century before. For emigrant Zoroastrians and more native Parsis, Bombay held the promise of opportunity and potential high prosperity. Khododad Irani was certainly no exception to the general sense of expectation, and thinking very much in terms of hard cash, he promptly found employment for both himself and his brother. By some means or other he persuaded Sheriar to accept the life of a wage-earner, although the dervish was reluctant to do so. He appears to have felt concerned for his brother's course in life however, and decided to stay with him in an attempt to educate him for the better. It seems that he wanted to prove to his brother that one could successfully acquit oneself at a mundane occupation without becoming a slave to the average impulses of greed and pleasure-seeking, a psychological arrangement which effectively prohibits higher development of the faculties. He strictly maintained his dietary habits as a teetotaller and vegetarian, and spent his leisure hours in contemplative solitude. While working for his employer, he even retained his dervish robe and his long hair. It was a highly idealistic approach on the part of this young Irani, still in his twenty-first year. Khododad was amazed, but though he respected his brother, he could make no serious attempt to understand Sheriar. He hoarded his wages, and could think only of earning more, of going into business, of earning a fortune, never again to be poor. That is how some peasants become tycoons, and arguably also, impervious to the fate of other peasants.

Sheriar's employer appears to have been a Parsi, and did not attempt to hide his dislike of a non-materialistic way of living. Undertones of conflict came to a climax after five months when the employer's manager picked a quarrel with the dervish. The latter was by now well aware that his efforts to produce a change in Khododad had failed. Wasting no time, he went to his boss and said that he was leaving, asking that his salary be paid over. His demand was respected, and with a magnanimous gesture he distributed all his money amongst some astonished servants at his lodging-house, a horrific action in the eyes of his parsimonious brother. Only two paltry *rupees* did he retain for the purpose of acquiring a wooden begging bowl and a simple staff. With these sparse possessions he started off on foot from Bombay to continue his dervishi. A baffled Khododad bade him farewell. What made the man wish to become a beggar in this land of promise?

The lesson was lost upon Khododad, but Sheriar never forgot his Bombay sojourn and all its implications. The maintenance of saintly externals means nothing, either in the outer or the inner worlds. It is not possible to change those who do not want to evolve.

Our traveller trekked northward through Gujerat in Western India. Here Parsis were concentrated in the Surat area, just as they were in the Bombay Presidency. He was dismayed to see the extent of their westernization; they were becoming a quasi-Asiatic breed of European. Families long domiciled in India had long ago lost their Persian roots in language and custom, but Hinduization was not westernization. Oddly enough, he would have felt more at home with Lieut.Col. H. Wilberforce Clarke, an engineer in the British Army who worked in Bengal, who was a member of the Royal Asiatic Society, and who translated into English the *Diwan* of Hafiz and other Persian works.

Other anomalies of cultural transplantation were visible in much of the professed dervish activity in India. The original dervish impetus which had arrived in the subcontinent during medieval times had largely spent itself even during the Mughal era. Hereditary *pirs* and tomb worship were very popular, if misleading.

Sheriar soon found that the Indian *sadhu* was frequently a glorified beggar in every sense of the phrase, and that it was easier for this category to gain public attention than their counterparts in Iran. In those days however, even gurus were poor, and Rishikesh may actually have harboured some *rishis*.

Setting his steps towards Cutch, his route passed through Ahmedabad. After a weary journey of several months, he reached the city of Karachi in Sind, a territory on the north-west borders of India (now in Pakistan). It is known that he stayed in Karachi for a month before disappearing again, but thereafter the thread of his journeying is lost to view. It was the beginning of ten long years of extensive wandering in India, an itinerary which he later said involved the endurance of hardships more severe than those he had experienced in Iran.

These wanderings in India are very largely a blank; the actual extent of his journeys remains vague, and their experiential content almost entirely limited to fragmentary reminiscences that appear either to have lost context or were perhaps even intended to be instructional. Though it was a comparative phase of freedom from persecution after the terrors of Qajar Persia, it would still require a considerable stretch of the imagination for the average armchair reader to project themselves into Sheriar's role and environment. Colourful it undoubtedly was, but also apt to be rugged and unpredictable. Sheriar was a foreigner in that he was neither a Hindu nor a Muslim; if he had any Zoroastrian acquaintances on his travels, they have completely escaped record.

Though the British definitely tolerated the natives, it was in a very condescending manner for the most part, and with an almost complete non-comprehension of native traditions which even the labours of scholars like Sir William Jones had done little to diminish. The representatives of the Raj would have seen nothing in a mendicant Irani other than another strange Easterner.

It is evident that Sheriar pronouncedly maintained his ascetic tendencies; if he got as much as one square meal every two days or so he probably considered it a feast of surfeit. He almost certainly maintained some form of contemplative exercise that would baffle the Khododads in whatever ethnic guise they might assume. He was very substantially an ascetic version of the *batini* phenomenon: the Iranian-based perspective of inward knowledge which has inspired, and been imitated by, a wide diversity of groupings reaching back into the distant pre-Islamic past, including Sassanian Mazdakites and the less salient Zurvanites of Achaemenian times.

Batinis are usually known in terms of grouping tendencies, but individual permutations were doubtless legion. The more common featural emphases and characteristics shared by numerous groupings have frequently been rendered extremely diffusely owing to factors of inadequate reporting, alienation of a specific grouping from social majorities, rivalry and copyism among different groupings, ethnic variations, diverse linguistic influences, repetition of some formats in a distorted and incomplete vehicle of expression.

One of the *batini* ingredients of teaching which varies markedly amongst detectable groups is that known as *tanasukh* or metempsychosis. Belief in the transmigration of souls has been a feature of several Shi'i sects, including the Ismailis, Druzes, and Nusairis. But for the historical delineation of this teaching, scholars like Carra De Vaux have been thrown back upon the testimonies of medieval Muslim authors who were often extremely biased against such belief. One interesting distinction which emerges is that while unorthodox groupings like the Yezidis of Kurdish Iran believe in a transmigration into the bodies of men and animals, the Ismailis did not admit the passage of the soul into animal bodies. While scholars have found difficulty with the subject, it is very feasible that many such beliefs are distortions of a fundamental belief in reincarnation that was quite widely in vogue in ancient times with similar confusions. Today, it is of course best known in India, where the popular idea is that the soul is liable to enter an animal body as punishment for misdeeds. A similar version is current amongst Buddhist sects.

Whatever *tanasukh* may have meant elsewhere, I have been able to ascertain that Sheriar (at least in his mature years) subscribed to it in its more logical form: he did not believe that the reincarnating human entity regresses into animal forms, though he did accept that animals were subject to reincarnation according to a different scale of evolution. He also quite definitely accepted that humans reap what they sow, with potentially drastic consequences.

To the materialist and others, all mention of reincarnation is of course nonsense, and the subject is even considered taboo. But logical reflection will conclude that this subject is no more illogical than the very vague ideas of oblivion which many moderns vaguely subscribe to on the authority of uncertainty over ultimates. A fair number of materialists have been known to find themselves inexplicably conscious while supposedly being clinically dead according to medical witnesses. If cardiac arrest is not in fact equivalent to death in every ostensibly fatal case, then even the most rabidly dogmatic might yet have cause to admit that they cannot be sure of what actually occurs in reality.

One possible reason for Sheriar's travels and travail in India may have been due to an assimilation of hearsay concerning certain "theosophical" trends achieving vogue at that time in Parsi India. During the nineteenth century certain texts had appeared in English and Persian which caught the attention of Parsi literati. Sheriar was as yet illiterate, but it would not be surprising if he had heard of these texts through Zoroastrian acquaintances in Bombay. He might well have decided that he wished to follow up cues to the experiential bases of such tradition, if at all possible. He may well have believed that the Kaivani tradition had not died out, and that since it had flourished in Mughal India, then Indian territory was still the best place to seek it.

At Bombay in 1818 had appeared an unusual book published by the Parsi savant Mulla Firuz Bin Kaus. It contained the text and English translation of a treatise known as the *Desatir*, a word which has been translated as "Ordinances." The full title of this work, as given by the publisher, is: *The Desatir or Sacred Writings of the Ancient Persian Prophets; in the Original Tongue; Together with the Ancient Persian Version and Commentary of the Fifth Sasan.* The manuscript had been brought from Iran by Mulla Kaus, the Parsi father of Mulla Firuz. The "Sacred Writings" were composed in a hybrid language that scholars deem to have been utilized for sectarian purposes. Components of both Indian and Iranian dialects are incorporated in this corpus of teachings attributed to fourteen pre-Islamic prophets commencing with the legendary Mahabad, and including Zarathushtra near the end of the series. The "Ancient Persian Version" was purportedly the work of the last of these prophets, who are depicted as part of a regular sequence that effectively revives the essential tradition of wisdom, a tradition which does not die but is distorted by heedless men. The teaching of this tradition was different to orthodox Zoroastrianism, e.g., Zarathushtra had employed allegorical devices in delivering Avestan scripture (the implication is that the allegorical ingredients were taken literally by formal religionists, but this is not a leitmotif of the *Desatir,* though certain scholars have tended to give this impression).

The *Desatir* was subsequently confused with theosophical trends of European and American idiom, bearing in mind that the Theosophical Society made its debut several decades later in the West. Ironically perhaps, the Theosophical claim of "hidden masters" more appropriately fits the Shia context for hidden *imams* (leaders) which had been current for over a thousand years. With respect to the *Desatir,* the allegorical subtlety of the *Avesta* goes back at least to the Sassanian era of Mazdak, and fits typical *batini* emphases.

Who produced the distinctive text of the *Desatir*? Boyce refers to it as a "literary forgery, produced probably within a Persian Sufi sect" (*Zoroastrians,* p. 197). Corbin more favourably inclined to the view that it was a product of the Kaivani school. This is strongly indicated in the teaching system of the *Desatir,* insofar as it can be called a system in its piecemeal literary expression. Reincarnation is stressed, with evolutionary progress achieved by contemplation and an ascetic aptitude of self-denial. Some have seen in it correspondences with Hindu ascetic practices, which does fit Kaivani associations, though these correspondences are not explicit. More explicit is the series of intermediate higher-than-human intelligences interposed between man and the aloof impersonal Absolute, a doctrine resembling a "Neoplatonic" format, though it could equally well be categorized in terms of ishraqi affiliation.

It is very difficult to say exactly how old the *Desatir* is, but it was probably no more of a forgery than much of the *Denkart* or the *Vendidad,* two of the major Zoroastrian scriptures which combine or conflate much myth and embellishment with fact, and with high-flown attributions that are clearly discernible. The Pahlavi-style language of the *Desatir* is perhaps indication enough that some enterprising linguist of the Akbarian era was attempting to inform a larger audience that *batini* emphases had been an equally viable vehicle of expression as orthodox interpretations. The artificer, or artificers, of the *Desatir* were quite possibly living in the shade of persecution or a preferable obscurity, not always conducive to frank and direct statement in plain English.

Publication of the *Desatir* did result in a strong wave of interest, and also some debates. The interest was still existent half a century later when Sheriar Irani passed through Bombay, and antagonism towards the "theosophical" trend was still strong in such neo-orthodox mouthpieces as Dastur Dhalla, Ph.D. and "High Priest of the Parsis" in twentieth century Karachi. Though an educated antiritualist himself, Dhalla disliked the more intensive indications implicit in the *Desatir* that Zoroastrianism had met with a blanketing by formalists. In his *History of Zoroastrianism*, Dhalla says that the *Dabistan-i-Mazahib* was written by Muhsin Fani in the seventeenth century, and drew the greater portion of its Zoroastrian materials from the *Desatir*. It is a great deal more accurate to state that the *Desatir* and *Dabistan* were part of the same tradition, though the *Desatir* was the earlier of the two works.

On the subject of authorship, an entry in the updated edition of the *Encyclopaedia of Islam* observes that for a long time Muhsin Fani was mistakenly thought to be the author of the Persian work known as the *Dabistan-i-Mazahib* (hereafter referred to as the *Dabistan* for convenience). Instead, "we must probably accept" the attribution in extant manuscripts to the pen of Mobad Shah, otherwise styled Mulla Mobad (the term *mobad* normally indicates membership of the Zoroastrian priestly class). Of this entity little is known, though it is certainly possible to agree that he was "an enlightened believer in the Parsi religion," as the entry abovementioned remarks.

Muhsin Fani of Kashmir was a seventeenth century writer of sufi associations, and reported to have been an associate of the liberal Mughal prince Dara Shikoh. Despite the supercession of the attribution to Fani's authorship, the *Dabistan* still has pronounced "sufi" associations, though not of the typical variety that attend upon the use of this very customary term.

The *Dabistan* was finished between 1654–7 in India. It achieved an erratic translation into English in 1843, and despite the lapse of nearly one and a half centuries, is still remarkably little known even as a pronouncedly liberal monument in the history of comparative religion and philosophy. It surveys no less than seven major religions and many more sects and traditions, including Zoroastrianism, Hinduism, Islam (both Sunni and Shia), Judaism, Christianity,

Tibetan Buddhism, Sikhism, Sufism, the Ismailis, and Greek philosophy. Its author was undeniably broad-minded, and from internal evidence of the text was born shortly before 1619 and resided at numerous places in India, including Agra, Lahore, and Kashmir. There are sufficient indications in the text to draw the strong conclusion that he was affiliated to the ishraqi sufi tradition associated with the name of Azar Kaivan, a sixteenth century Zoroastrian who emigrated from Safavid Iran to North India during the reign of Akbar.

The *Dabistan* is the main source for the life of Azar Kaivan. Writing earlier than Dhalla, the Parsi scholar J.J. Modi observed that it was Sir William Jones who early attributed the authorship of this book to Muhsin Fani, though other scholars had seen the error of this judgment, which was based upon a mere quotation from Fani at the beginning of the *Dabistan*. Modi inferred (very debateably) that the author had come to India from Iran during his childhood, and feasibly estimates the latter's date of birth at *c*.1615. The author of the *Dabistan* relates that in 1618, one of Azar Kaivan's disciples known as Mobad Hushiyar, carried him as a child to receive the blessings of a famous yogi known as Balk Natha. It is evident that this seventeenth century comparativist grew up in a milieu of cosmopolitan influences fostered by the Kaivani grouping. Modi suggested that the effective author was none other than Farzaneh Behram ibn Farhad Aspandiyar Parsi, a learned Irani Zoroastrian versed in Persian and Arabic, and a close disciple of Azar Kaivan. This suggestion was proffered despite the conceded fact that the individual in question is mentioned in the third person in the *Dabistan* list of Kaivan's disciples. Modi remarks that we should not judge the ways of antique authors by modern standards. Anonymous authorship does make for a decrease of ego perhaps, as with pseudonyms, but disparities in dating would mean that a second party must have redrafted the notes of Farzaneh Behram if he was so closely involved, since Modi himself writes that Farzaneh Behram ibn Farhad died in 1624 at Lahore.

It is perhaps applicable enough to observe with Modi that

the *Dabistan* is not original in some of its contents, but more of a compilation. From what the author himself says, it is evident that he encountered learned representatives of the Hindus, Jews, Zoroastrians, Christians, Muslims, and others. The section on the Zoroastrians is very unorthodox, referring to many obscure sects and citing a substantial number of writings by *mobads* and others, including a commentary on the poetical writings of Azar Kaivan. Writing some three centuries later, Modi stated that only a few of these sources (over twenty of them) were known to him. One such was the *Desatir,* of uncertain age, though Modi wrote that it appears to be a late medieval work, at least in its present form.

Modi deemed the *Desatir* to be "sufistic to a certain extent", and followed the British scholar Erskine in considering it a derivative of the Persian sufis and the ascetic practices of yogis. For the stress on *ahimsa* (non-violence) and asceticism is pronounced, and sufficient to evoke Modi's accompanying description in terms of Hindu-Buddhistic tendencies. This apparent eclecticism is a feature of the Kaivani tradition, providing it is understood that the eclecticism was not theoretical but experiential, and not random adoption of different practices but a very disciplined approach to cultural exigencies of that era. Late Akbarian India and post-Akbarian India were in increasing danger of influences from anti-liberal extremists. The antagonism to Greek philosophy on the part of orthodox Muslims arguably left the way open to an escalation of bigotry against the indigenous inhabitants of India. One Kaivani objective seems to have been to counteract this trend; men like Farzaneh Behram ibn Farhad specifically incorporated Greek philosophy while also utilizing Hindu and other native Indian elements. That they were also aware that there was much superstition and hypocrisy present in varied beliefs is indicated by such statements from the author of the *Dabistan* that he would attempt to give some account of the knowledge, work and manners of the ancients and the moderns, as reported by those perceptive enough to see what is obscured by the worshippers of outward forms and the arbitrary choosers of inner meaning;

all this was proffered without hatred or jealousy and without corroborating or refuting.

Such perspectives were entirely lost upon Dhalla, the high priest of Karachi, who disapprovingly refers to the Zoroastrian mystics of Kaivan's era who were dissatisfied with formal religion. While Dhalla might have been able to understand their indifference to ritual observances, he laments that literal interpretation failed to meet their longings. Dhalla did not like the *Dabistan,* finding its statements uncorroborated by the writings of the Zoroastrian priests (remembering that Dhalla adhered to the Muhsin Fani attribution). He observes that Kaivani era works which purport to be translations into Persian from the original Pahlavi in actuality mostly reproduced Greek philosophy current in Mughal India via Arabic versions. One wonders how else far-reaching thinkers could have provoked narrow thinkers and high priests to look at Greek philosophy; or to put the matter in different words, if there was some coincidence of content in ancient times between Greek and Iranian philosophical variants, then the common denominator might prove indigestible to preconceived ideas of uniqueness.

When Sheriar Irani was in Bombay during the mid-1870's, he may well have encountered Parsi enthusiasts who were collecting anything resembling a Kaivani text; some of these enthusiasts were probably future candidates for the high-flown interpretations of European and American Theosophy. Sheriar would have seen that such people were mainly armchair enthusiasts. What could they hope to do merely through books? he would doubtless have thought. Features of his lifestyle at Bombay strongly suggest that he was already conversant with Kaivani teachings, perhaps even from his Iranian wanderings; he was conceivably trying to demonstrate to the sceptical that a Kaivani ascetic could acquit himself in mundane affairs. He himself no doubt thought in retrospect that he had been too demonstrative at this stage.

It is my contention that he was an effective Kaivani, or the nearest sequel to the prototype that one can find in nineteenth century Parsi annals. The Kaivanis can be classified as a type of sufi, but it is probably equally accurate to say that they were a distinctive variant of the ancient *batini* momentum that quite possibly goes back to the second millenium B.C. if the earlier of the dates posited for Zarathushtra is correct.

At the time of writing, detailed informative sources in English on the Kaivanis are notably scarce. A recent synopsis of Zoroastrian religious history by an eminent scholar entirely omits reference to Azar Kaivan; the best monograph on the subject was written half a century ago and is accessible only in the best library stocks of learned journals; even the flawed and cumbersome English translation of the *Dabistan* is now rare; even Corbin, who was sympathetic to the Kaivani tradition, referred to it only in passing. I will attempt to redress the balance of bias and neglect.

Sheriar's initially known destination of Karachi was another Parsi living centre, and it is possible that he may have hoped to find some further clue there to current events in the Kaivani idiom. Did the Kaivani grouping still exist in India? This was a question that was feasibly prominent in his mind. North India was the most obvious area for our transplanted dervish to investigate in this respect, since that region had been the scene for sixteenth and seventeenth century Kaivani events, from Kashmir and the Punjab to Kaivan's abode at Patna in Bihar. To Sheriar at any rate, such a quest would have been only one aspect of his itinerary, since solitary contemplation was one of the Kaivani ideals.

The threadbare details of his travels tend to underline the fact that Sheriar was not one of those stentorian mystics who declare their memoirs to all and sundry. Everything I have heard about him indicates that he was reticent and even evasive about matters that were of deep import to him.

In his later years he would relate an episode which reputedly occurred during his Indian wanderings. Walking through a desert, he developed a painful open sore on the sole of his foot. He was also overcome by thirst, and began to feel that he could not walk any further, always a danger in desert terrain. Repeating a sacred name, he continued on until he swooned. When he recovered consciousness, he saw before him a venerable old man and a youth. They were carrying leather water bags, from which they appeased the wayfarer's burning thirst. The patriarch spoke to him, saying words to the effect of: "Why have you come here? Why should you trouble God by acting foolishly?" He told the traveller to continue on until he came to a hut occupied by an old man who would give him some food, and also directed him to the nearest town. Feeling revived, Sheriar made ready to go. Turning to thank his benefactors he found that they had mysteriously disappeared; the vast stretch of sand before him was devoid of life. Kneeling down in gratitude, he offered a prayer.

Upon arrival at the hut he had been informed of, the occupant presented him with a loaf of bread. Eating half of it, the traveller placed the remainder in his begging bowl and went on his way. Presently he reached a wide river that he was unable to cross, never having learnt to swim; but without losing heart he rested on the banks and soon fell asleep. He was awakened by the peal of camel bells, and espied a caravan approaching the riverside. He enquired of the merchants as to how they intended to ford the river, and they replied that they would cross by camel-back. So he asked if they would take him with them. For this service they demanded a sum of two *rupees,* and when he told them that he was destitute, they refused to take him. Dusk approached, and the dervish was still wondering how he was going to cross the waters. His faith in a providential assistance did not waver. Feeling hungry, he took out the remaining piece of bread from his bowl. At that moment he saw a shoal of fish swarming by the edge of the water where he sat; unmindful of his hunger, he broke the bread into crumbs and threw these to the fish. At this juncture he heard a voice close by asking "What are you doing here?" Glancing up, he noticed a tall and stout figure standing near him. When the stranger heard of his plight, he erupted into laughter and said, "Why, there is no need for you to go through the waters. *There* lies the way to the town, you blind man! Come, I will guide you." To his surprise, the dervish now perceived a strip of terra firma above water-level which stretched the full width of the river; it was the first time he had seen it. He followed the stranger across the ford, but when he tried to express thanks, he was rebuked with the words "It is not I you have to thank." Reaching the opposite bank, the guide said: "Come with me. I shall myself take you to the town." Darkness had fallen by this time, and in about half an hour they reached the streets of a town. The guide took his companion to a shop and left him there, and after his departure was seen no more. A little later the dervish was dumbfounded to hear that this township was sixty miles away from the river they had crossed, and yet the distance had been covered by he and his guide on foot in thirty minutes.

This tale has been construed as an example of aid bestowed by persons having access to supernatural powers. But sufi types have been known to conceal their development experiences in the form of symbolical stories. From this perspective, Sheriar's anecdote might be interpreted as an allegory conveying the substance of his inner life during that period.

Part of the reason for his subsequent reticence on the subject of his wandering was owing to his perception of how little the average brain can understand outside its immediate train of associations, a discrepancy which all too frequently causes puzzlement, hostility, belittling condecension, or downright shock. He liked to relate an anecdote which he ascribed to the fifth year of his Indian dervishi, when he was travelling once again through Gujerat. He came to a dense forest that was reputed to be haunted, and running alongside of which was a broad, muddy stream. People in the vicinity had warned him not to enter the forest, but having gained a certain fearlessness with regard to local superstitions, he set out to do so. But however much he walked through this forest, he repeatedly found himself back at the point from which he started. Seeing his labours to be of no avail, he next tried to cross the stream, but half-way over his guiding staff sank deep into the mud. He stood in prayer, and subsequently managed to reach the other side without further accident. Walking towards a nearby group of men, he saw them flee in terror; as none ever came from that direction, they assumed him to be the ghost of the forest. Only one of them did not retreat, and after an exchange of words, he took the dervish to his hut, gave him some buttermilk, and set him safely on his way.

One item of his dervish regalia was a knife which he carried on his person for emergency purposes. He was grateful for its presence on the occasion when he despatched an attacking cobra with this weapon; the incident took place in a jungle, where he was companioned by three other mendicants, all of whom took to their heels at the time.

Though something of an *ahimsa* idealist, Sheriar was also a realist in having learnt the hard way that not everything under the heavens can be viewed as an unmitigated blessing, particularly if it is venomous.

He found that it was extremely difficult to find quality instructors in the experiential field to which he had committed himself. Every fool who has a vision or hallucination generally tends to think that he (or she) is an authority upon invisible hierarchies and similar matters of convenient vagueness. Even an illiterate could gain information concerning great teachers of the past, but where was the continuation into his own time? He could view stupendous ruins and visit famous shrines, but these do not produce illumination, and sometimes were too crowded even for tourists. There were plenty of orders and cults to choose from, but a freethinker did not always want the attendant obeisance routine of conformity even when it was ethnically liberal. He was certainly not content with the fetishism that was so common amongst Indian *faqirs*. The stark reality of his own experiences (apart from any question of dedication) tended to insulate him from the emotionalism which the more shallow "sufi" *faqirs* indulged in, just as he was unmoved by the false tranquillity of those *sadhus* who were (and are) nothing more than hemp addicts.

As a Zoroastrian *uwaysi,* he was largely unconcerned with the long-standing controversy amongst dervish orders over adaptation to Hindu attitudes. He was sensitive to the best in the Hindu field, just as he was sensitive to the best in other traditions, without being blind to the far-reaching and cumbersome effects of distortions. He may even have grasped that the mutated Vedic religion had some close parallels with the Zoroastrian heritage.

The man who was shortly to become the Vedantic exponent of the century was still attending Calcutta University when Sheriar was travelling the country. Narendra Nath Datta, alias Swami Vivekananda (d.1902), who was likewise to journey extensively as a mendicant, evinced a distinctive capacity for assimilating the intrinsic significance of the past. He stood amongst the same Mughal remains that Sheriar saw, and could so closely align their part in the Indian historical phenomenon along with earlier cultures that he astonished Western pupils with the sheer intensity of his Mughal reveries. Vivekananda's affinities with our Persian dervish were stronger than might at first be inferred from his ultimate fame as a Hindu patriot. He was brought up on quotations from Hafiz by his father, an attorney in the Calcutta High Court who had adopted certain Islamic manners and customs. His leading Indian pupil Sadananda was a native of Islamic Jaunpur, reared to a Persian education heavily flavoured with sufi ideas; Sister Christine Greenstidel writes of these two *faqirs*: "When they recited sufi poetry, they were sufis." The same American pupil relates how Vivekananda would talk for hours at a time of the Prophet Muhammad, correcting the erroneous ideas of bigoted Americans. Vivekananda's characteristic repetition of "*Azad*!" ("the Free") was not of course a Hindu habit, but of sufi origin.

Vivekananda was effectively (though not historically) the first of the Hindu efflux towards Western shores, whose example practically all subsequent gurus, yogis and swamis have attempted to emulate in some form or other. While his contribution in the 1890's was an appropriate stimulant to Victorian thought, the spate of twentieth century copyists amounts to bandwagon theatricals.

While Vivekananda tended to concentrate upon the Indian inter-cultural phenomenon from the angle of the subcontinent itself, Sheriar Irani tended to think in terms of the influences which had infiltrated from outside areas. Western scholars were even then proving that most of the densely piled ethnic layers in India came from the vast migration area of Central Asia, a racial exodus sequence which includes the Aryans of Vedic times and the much more recent Mughals. Sheriar was more alive to the dervish influx which had been occurring for over a thousand years.

One exceptional feature in Vivekananda's psychology which Sheriar did not incorporate in his own career was the assimilation of modern Western science. But then this was rare among both Hindus and Muslims, and it has to be said that some contemporary British and American expositions of the 1890's read drably by comparison with some of Vivekananda's more animated metaphysico-scientific comments. An intrigued Robert Ingersoll attempted to fathom the Swami's views on the *atman*; though the former was an agnostic and a stern critic of religous ideologies, he was sympathetic to the Hindu firebrand and cautioned him to be careful in preaching new ideas and outspoken criticisms of the native ways of life and thought in America. Ingersoll explained that only fifty years earlier, a visitor like Vivekananda would have been hanged or even burned alive, and added that even if he had arrived much later, the native response would have been to stone him out of the villages.

Sheriar Irani had known this kind of xenophobia at firsthand in Iran, and appropriately enough perhaps, never in his life made any specific attempt at preaching.

One of Sheriar's guarded reminiscences of his Indian dervishi concerned an old man he discovered in the hills, seated in obvious contemplation. The patriarch opened his eyes, and asked the dervish what he wanted. He seemed pleased with the reply, "I want nothing." Indian saints are often plagued with requests for miracles and assistance in mundane objectives; even other holy men sometimes desire from their peers and superiors diverse forms of status reassurance.

Whether this encounter involved a Muslim or Hindu, and whether it may have taken place in the Himalayas, are now matters for guesswork. There is no definite indication that he ever actually entered Himalayan terrain, long considered sacred by Hindu ascetics. Kashmir had Kaivani associations, and may well have excited his attention for that reason. As a Zoroastrian he would doubtless have been fascinated by Islamic legends centring upon Balkh which linked Zarathushtra with this ancient city of Central Asia, just north of the Hindu Kush mountains. Such legend has been preserved in Firdausi's *Shahnama*, a major Iranian poetic work of some vintage. While it is possible that Zarathushtra's patron Kavi Vishtaspa reigned in the Balkh locale of ancient Bactria, it has so far proved impossible to substantiate this. Whether Sheriar's fascination for tradition could lure him into this region remains conjectural, but there were some serious deterrents to an expedition into the Afghan highlands owing to the formidable terrain and the warlike nature of the inhabitants. Sheriar is likely to have been hesitant at the prospect of entering this stronghold of Sunni Islam, where tribal, national, and religious feeling were high. Beyond Balkh and the Oxus (Amu Darya) river were cities like Bukhara and Samarkand, places which had similarly amassed manifold associations in sufi history. Since the Mongol invasions, this whole area of Central Asia had remained almost inaccessible to non-Islamic visitors and enemies alike. The British had drawn rein at the North-West Frontier of India, aghast at the resisting fury of the Pathan tribes. Far to the north, the Russians were even now pressing in the opposite direction against the nomadic obstacles that guarded Turkestan.

A decisive event in Central Asian history occurred two-thirds of the way through Sheriar Irani's Indian dervishi, something of which it is possible he heard of at the time. In January 1881 occurred the battle of Geok Tepe in Turkestan, in which the last Turkoman tribe to hold out against the Tzarist advance were decisively beaten. These were the Tekkes, reputedly the most fierce of the Turkomans. The tribal power was ruthlessly crushed in what was known as annexation, and Turkestan became part of Russia, the area being thrown open to Western commercialism. To some extent, there was a cultural migration south of the Oxus into the remote wilds of Afghanistan, new villages appearing south of the borderline which was agreed upon in 1884. The cities of old Turkestan were to live on as twentieth century tourist spots, though somewhat altered in appearance; Tashkent was almost completely destroyed by an earthquake in 1966.

Even if one could precisely ascertain the movements of our dervish, many Western and Eastern investigators alike would find serious difficulties in adjusting to many of the mental perspectives of the subject. Exactly whose view would be etic and whose emic might be rather difficult to succinctly state, particularly since modern varieties of eticism differ more than slightly. As regards Sheriar, for instance, if he had been reliably informed of Tekke history (which is quite possible), he would have known that the Tekke tribesmen were notorious in northeastern Iran for their slaveraiding exploits. He may even have witnessed such raids upon Iranian villages, when hapless inhabitants were carried off by force to a very uncertain fate. It may have been more difficult for him to learn, and to accept, that slaves were considered essential for agriculture in some Central Asian regions; the slaves of the Turkomans not only went to the estates of the tribal khans but also to the *ulama*. Apart from such niceties as to who was ultimately to blame, Sheriar is likely to have adopted the view that cause-effect ratios are actually finer to elucidate than contracted variants commonly known in the popular Hindu karmic model. Some Hindus have tried to explain that there are different kinds of karmic cause-effect trains with differing repercussion rates, views that have not been particularly well understood in popular Western consumption of the *karma* concept (with results in the idiom of indigestion that sweepingly equates "self-realization" with the sexual experience, in flat contradiction to a more than superficial knowledge of the purported philosophy).

It is evident that Sheriar accepted metampsychosis in a Kaivani manner, though not in the format described in the *Desatir*. To him, after being exposed to the horrors of persecution and the Babi tales of torture, it understandably must have seemed that the only just and orderly scheme in the universe was one in which the cruel themselves reaped their own cruelty at some crucial point. A materialist might laugh, but for all he knows, by his own standards of nihilism, it could even be true (particularly when logically viewed against the standards of disorderliness imposed by materialist schemes of chance and sheer coincidence; materialistic determinism is more orderly, but arguably employs truncated logic). The persecutors who rammed wads of cloth down the throats of Babi victims with mallets, were in Sheriar's view, asking for very serious repercussions even if they did believe they were destined for paradise after one lifespan in which they did just as they wanted. If the Kaivanis are even partially right, then "hell" must be very complex and sophisticated by comparison with dullard standards. If modern cases of the cardiac arrest phenomenon have some viable extension – a phenomenon in which the body is clinically dead but the subject transpires to possess vivid consciousness – then a lot of people might be in for some surprises when everything is supposedly over. Even those (pseudo)scientists who mercilessly torture stolen pets and wild life in the most diabolical manner in the name of progress (and salary) may feel sharp pangs of unrequited conscience in the possible light of an increased empirical extension of consciousness when least expected.

Contrary to materialist and theological dogmatists alike, Sheriar did not attempt to impose his views upon others. Quite typical of his psychology is an instance narrated in the commentary of the "Fifth Sasan" to the ordinances of Zarathushtra as preserved in the *Desatir*:

A sage whose name is rendered as Chengerengacheh came from India to Balkh in order to seek out Zarathushtra, the prophet of Yazdan. Before he could speak a single word or ask any question, the prophet told him: "Commit not to your tongue what you have in your heart, but keep it secret." Chengerengacheh duly became a follower of Avestan teaching, and returned to India, admired by the *mobads* ("wise men") on account of his wisdom (See Mulla Firuz trans., pp. 125–6).

In the tenth and last year of his Indian travels, the eighteenth of his dervishi as a whole, Sheriar Irani psychologically reached a point of acute crisis. He was overwhelmingly aware that he had not reached his inner objective. It was *circa* 1884 when he decided upon a desperate measure in an attempt to clarify his awareness of depth matters. This took the form of a very strict version of a famous sufi discipline, involving forty days of meditation intended to lead up to a condition of illumination in those capable of it.

I have seen reports which assume that this discipline was yogic-inspired, but it was far more likely to have been of Iranian derivation in this case, since it was in fairly common vogue in Qajar Iran at that time. Sheriar adopted it in its extreme form as attested in Iran. E.G. Browne met individuals who regarded this discipline as a magical powers stunt – that is, some practitioners hoped to gain psychic powers from the practice. It is perhaps no wonder that practitioners were reported to experience horrifying hallucinations while gradually reducing their food intake to nil, while sitting immobile in a carefully marked off spot. Yogis did practise something very similar, and with the same mixed motives varying with individuals. Sheriar's version was conscientiously severe, and not undertaken for the acquisition of powers.

This discipline was also known in Sunni communities of dervishes, particularly in India. It was often associated with the Prophet Muhammad's contemplative retreats to a cave on Mount Hira near Mecca, where he is said to have spent a month of every year as a *hanif*. Islam commemorates this in the fasting month known as Ramadan, during which food is taken only between sunset and sunrise in accordance with Quranic injunction. Probably in closer accord with such precedent, dervishes have frequently added seclusion and nocturnal vigils to a fasting programme, with forty days and nights as a recognized objective. Aflaki's *Munaqib al-Arifin* reports that Rumi underwent several such sessions during his highly disciplined training.

While Rumi adopted an indoor setting (the use of an isolated room or a mosque was common in Sunni environs), our hardy Irani dervish selected an outdoor location in a deep jungle. He appears to have marked out a circle upon the ground near the banks of a convenient river, his aim being to sit within the confines of this consecrated boundary, without either solid food or sleep, for the desired forty days and nights.

According to his later report, he counted thirty days after commencing this rigorous programme, subsisting on water.

His awareness became acutely introverted, and he encountered some alarming experiences of the kind which would now be called "occult," but which are rarely understood. Their nature apart, they can represent grave psychological dangers to the unwary subject. Our subject's force of mind and inbuilt tenacity carried him through these experiences, but the tremendous strain upon his physical organism forced him to desist after achieving three-quarters of the time schedule. Still he seemed no nearer to the elusive enlightenment for which he had struggled so persistently. His body emaciated after the lengthy ordeal, and feeling overwhelmingly disheartened at having to stop short of the time limit, he fell asleep from sheer exhaustion at the riverside. He had not allowed himself sleep for a whole month, discounting any inadvertent doze.

During this respite, according to his later report, he had a vivid dream which influenced him strongly. Exactly how he viewed this dream is not clear, and it would seem that caution is required before assuming (as was later done) that it was this dream which made him go to Bombay. I am by no means certain that we have the full report of this episode, and nor do we have his exact words on the subject as reported. In this dream he was told by some entity that he would not be able to achieve what he sought, that he should return home, that he would have a son who would achieve the objective.

It is undeniable that this experience as a whole made a deep impact upon him. It later provided a rationale of precedent for the devotional movement centring upon his famous son Merwan Sheriar (alias Meher Baba), whose fame totally eclipsed that of his father. In the process, the forbear's life was inordinately simplified.

The *irfani* (gnostic) philosophers of Safavid and Qajar Iran maintained much earlier views in their interpretation of dreams, views with which Sheriar is likely to have been familiar. There were said to be three basic varieties of dream experience: (1) dreams caused by bodily discomfort and similar disturbance, of absolutely no value; (2) dreams amounting to an impressional overflow from the waking state, again valueless and potentially misleading; (3)

dreams worthy of interpretation, a very few being precognitive, but most being figurative and requiring elucidation accordingly. This schema bears little or no relation to Jungian analyses of collective archetypes and similar theories; in the qualified irfani-ishraqi perspective, to interpret virtually all dreams in accordance with generalized ideational meanings and standard symbolism is nothing less than nonsense. Different minds select different associative triggers even for the same informational content. Someone's blatherskite may be someone else's blunderbuss, to use plain English.

Sheriar Irani did make his way to Bombay, the place from where he had started out upon his wanderings in India ten years before. There he expected to find his sister Piroja, whom he knew to have emigrated to India.

Whatever the reason for his return to the beaten track of former associations, he did not at any point intend to relinquish his efforts at clarification of the consciousness. Though his thirty days of denial were later to be viewed as a symptom of the inadequacy of ascetic endeavour, he himself viewed the attempt as a crucial catalyst. To some it merely represents a horrifying ordeal, particularly for armchair enthusiasts.

Where were the Kaivanis? It seems that Sheriar grasped that he had to become one.

It transpired that his sister Piroja was living in Poona, a city about 120 miles inland from Bombay. When he at last found her residence, she was overjoyed to see him after their long separation, during which time she had lost all hope of meeting him again. He stayed with her for some length of time, though leading a withdrawn life. Piroja was afraid that he would disappear again, and kept pleading with him to marry and settle down. But his invariable reply was to the effect that he intended to return to his wandering vocation of dervishi.

He was like a fish out of water amongst the increasingly westernized Parsi community in which his sister lived. Piroja and others had no interest in higher reaches of the mind. Their form of Sunday religion sufficed their notions of a continued existence after death. His sister lived on domestic talk, and to her sufis were merely something vaguely connected with the detestable Muslims whom she had learned to abhor on the distant Yazd plain. She may well have heard of Kaivanis, but to her even this subject would have meant nothing but old books. Sheriar felt suspended in a social void; how could he live with all this small talk for the rest of his life?

The anxious, well-meaning Piroja seized every opportunity to persuade her brother in the direction of marriage. While they were talking of this repetitive subject one day, the six year old daughter of a Zoroastrian neighbour walked past the front door on her way to school, holding a writing slate under her arm. This child was the daughter of Piroja's friend Golendoon, the wife of an Irani called Dorabji Khooramshahi. The latter was a native of Khooramshah as the name indicates; his family had recently emigrated to India, and his daughter Shirin had been born a few days after their landing in Bombay.

So persistent were the pleas of Piroja that Sheriar thought to put an end to her daily matrimonial talk once and for all. He had a sudden idea, so piercing that he impulsively rendered it into action. Pointing to the little girl outside, he said (approximately) to his sister with an air of finality, "Alright, if I marry, I will marry that little girl; or else I will never marry." He appears to have voiced this assertion with complete trust in the thought that he had uttered a ridiculous and impossible proposal, to which the parents of the girl would surely never agree. But he did not take into account the tenacity of his sister. Piroja took his ultimatum very seriously, and visited her friend Golendoon. Relating the delicate complexities of the situation, she begged and implored consent to the betrothal of Sheriar and the girl Shirin. She emphasized that Golendoon alone could "save" her brother from returning to the mendicant life. Golendoon's feelings were swayed by her friend's anxiety, and to add to this, she had developed a respect for the proposed husband. The result was that she agreed to the match. When Shirin's father Dorabji learned that his six year old daughter had been promised in marriage to an ascetic, he vented explosive anger upon his wife. But when his temper cooled, he felt that a word of honour could not be broken, and so finally he accepted the unusual arrangement.

As for the dervish himself, the news of his future marriage fell upon his ears with the shock of a thunderbolt. Stupefied at the effect of his hasty utterance, his first impulse may well have been to flee. But having given his word to Piroja, he felt that he could not now withdraw. (The code of honour amongst Irani Zoroastrians was of very high standard, with a promise being considered as a sacred obligation). So the dervish became engaged, and it was agreed that the marriage should take place when the girl came of age.

Sheriar now applied his will to a new role in life. In this he was exercising the well attested post-dervishi scope of adaptability, grafting a complementary development upon the foundation of his past labours.

The Parsi community of Poona looked with interest upon their new recruit. The more affluent and successful smiled condescendingly at the phenomenon of this ascetic or whatever he was – a man in his prime who had no money, no standing in society, no business, no home of his own, whose betrothed was not even of age. Well, of course one had to sympathize with emigrants from Iran who had been through rough times, but what was the point in asceticism? What was he really? Just an uneducated labourer.

Sheriar smiled back. They would all be dead in thirty or forty years, with nothing to show for their imagined superiority but bleached bones at the local tower of silence, such bones as he had contemplated every day of his childhood.

It was true enough that he had to start from scratch. He was still practically illiterate, and possessed virtually nothing but a dervish robe. Yet he had acquired unusual abilities of concentration, alertness, and perseverance. He also knew that the adaptable dervish can do better in the world than the worldly, if he puts his mind to it.

His choice of occupation was indeed limited to the manual variety. Having lived so close to nature, he had a fair knowledge of trees and plants, and so decided to take up gardening. In those days British-occupied Poona was famous for its well-cultivated gardens, and many large houses needed the services of a horticulturist. He made his debut as a gardening apprentice, but soon graduated to prestige as head gardener at a number of mansions. He earned well and after a while went into business, acquiring a teashop, those Eastern versions of cafes. The venture proved financially successful.

Meanwhile he had been formally educating himself, learning to read and write his native language of Persian, together with the local Gujarati script used by the Parsis. More remarkable was his determination to master Arabic, a venture in which he was also successful. Most literate Parsis never studied Arabic, and many of them were not well-read in Persian, which they did not require for either religious or mundane purposes. Sheriar was clearly following a Kaivani precedent, which had exhibited a high standard of learning and specifically incorporated Arabic into its unofficial curriculum. Sheriar was not merely desirous of reading Zoroastrian religious works, but also wanted to research diverse sufi classics and related treatises. He did in fact become something of a scholar in both Persian and Arabic, and would certainly have been able to hold his own in educated circles save in the more elite echelon of manuscript scholars. There were very few Parsis who bothered to acquire his linguistic range. During his earlier years he must have very often heard quotations from the *Mathnavi* (of Rumi) and various *diwans*, not to mention the *Avesta* and the *Quran*; now he had the opportunity to see for himself what the texts said.

After eighteen years of unremitting practical application to what is known in Arabic as the *tariqa* (path), he was perhaps better able to investigate the complex literary areas of "sufism" than some Ph.D's. Sheriar had also acquired the knowledge that texts are not the ultimate referee. For him, oral tradition and experience in the field came first, not second.

What literature was readily available to him? Orthodox Zoroastrian texts in Gujarati were now easy to obtain, and classical Persian sufi books were not difficult to seek out in

Bombay. Not a few Parsis were fascinated by the Kaivani works, and since the mid-nineteenth century, these works had been eagerly sought after and translated by Parsis who were encouraged by Sir Jamshetji Jejeebhoy, a well known Parsi philanthropist who was liberal with funds. For instance, the *Dabistan* cites a commentary on the poetical writings of Azar Kaivan by Mobad Khuda Jui; it was known as the *Jam-i-Khaikhushru*, and the Persian text of this was published in 1848 at the instigation of Jejeebhoy. The author's name, as Modi explains, means one in search of God; he was a disciple of Kaivan. (This treatise is also known as *Mukashafat-i-Kaivan,* the "Revelations of Kaivan").

It is interesting to discover what the Parsis were writing about Kaivan at the time Sheriar was commencing his text studies. In 1888 was published at Bombay the *Parsi Prakash,* edited by B.B. Patel, an orthodox Parsi scholar. This Gujarati work on Parsi history described Azar Kaivan, the son of Azar Goshasp, as a learned Persian priest who believed in a universal religion, who spent twenty-eight years in meditation and then came to India from Iran; he settled at Patna where he became known as a teacher of a universal creed, and died at Patna in 1614 at the age of eighty-five.

It is now more accurate to state that there is no proof that Kaivan was of priestly background, though he does appear to have been both learned and poetical. His universal teaching was not so much a doctrine, but a perspective that was passed on to his disciples and followers with varying degrees of clarity in comprehension. It was not easy to get to know Kaivan.

Williams Jackson has left the information that a learned Irani of his acquaintance in Yazd, one Khodabaksh Rais, thought of Azar Kaivan as a "half Brahman, half Zoroastrian, a believer in metempsychosis." This was in 1903, after Khodabaksh and a few other scholars had been to Bombay; these scholars encouraged the younger generation of Irani students at Yazd to maintain close contact with the Parsis. All the more important Zoroastrian manuscripts had been sent to India in the interests of safety, but Jackson urged upon the Yazd Iranis the importance of a careful search, particularly among the older families, for texts that had possibly been overlooked.

In reading the *Desatir,* Sheriar would have found it clearly stated that there are two basic types of seeker after truth, which the commentary states are both "distinguished as the enlightened and the guides." One type are designated as *hirtasp,* whose lifestyle is one of ascetic self-denial. The second type are designated as *sirdasp,* who also practise *ahimsa* and good works, but whose lifestyle does not involve the practise of austerities and solitary seclusion; this type investigate the real nature of things by the guidance of reason (Mulla Firuz – Erskine trans., p. 23).

This "Mahabadian" distinction might be aligned with the two major aspects of Sheriar's life pattern, though the second one took some time to mature no doubt, while the first requires its own extension of maturity.

Another work available for study was the *Sharistan-i chahar chaman,* written by Kaivan's disciple Farzaneh Behram ibn Farhad, a Zoroastrian ishraqi who was fluent in both Persian and Arabic like several other contemporary Kaivanis. Ishraqi teaching was not particularly well understood by most nineteenth century Parsis, who were insulated from the experiential code involved. Sheriar Irani was an exception, and would have been one of those who most appreciated the description of Azar Kaivan as the "king or leader of the *ishraqi* philosophers," to borrow Modi's version of a statement by Khuda Jui in the abovementioned commentary on the writings of Kaivan. This was an indication of the continuation from the trend nominally originating with Sohravardi Maqtul of the twelfth century.

The Khuda Jui commentary dilates upon such themes as visions and dreams, the art of recovering from ecstatic conditions and imbalances, and the art of separating the soul from the body. These topics are subject to fabulation by beginners and self-seeking parties. The author relates that he wrote this commentary at the request of several "Yazdanians." This was a broad term of reference to Zoroastrians practising the esoteric aspect of the Avestan religion, persons who did believe that there were states of mind not accessible to orthodox confines but which needed regulation, and who did believe in the existence of a soul but accepted that this entity does not automatically develop itself or graduate to salvation by the assistance of mere belief or mere "good works."

In 1879 a work known as *Ayin-i Hushang* (The Religion of Hushang) was published in Bombay as a result of the labours of the Zoroastrian scholar Mirza Bahram Rustom Nasrabadi, who wrote an introduction to four Persian treatises in which ishraqi influence is apparent. These treatises emanated from the circle of Azar Kaivan's disciples. This "Zoroastrian ishraqi" literature was dubbed the religion of Hushang owing to the prominence of the legendary prophet of that name in Kaivani lore, a kind of shorthand for the religion within a religion which the Kaivanis claimed as their heritage, in addition to their more cosmopolitan extension of alignment with the essentials of other religions and sects. Zoroastrian ishraqis effectively proved the assertion of Sohravardi Maqtul that the ishraqi philosophical tradition had indrawn more ancient Zoroastrian elements; it might be said that Zoroastrian philosophers never forgot Maqtul for remembering them. The fact of a number of them pursuing the study of Arabic was a consequence of Maqtul's thorough acquaintance with this Semitic language, in which he wrote his more technical philosophical treatises; in Maqtul's day Persian was becoming a fully revived tongue amongst Iranian Muslims, but the Greek philosophical tradition (an important aspect of ishraqi studies and teaching) had been mediated through the Arabic linguistic channel for several centuries.

Even long after Maqtul, the Shia Muslim ishraqis tended to write their technical treatises in Arabic, a language increasingly inaccessible to popular readership. Even by the seventeenth century, Mulla Sadra Shirazi (d.1640) wrote only one work in Persian, entitled *Sa Asl,* which as Bayat comments, is so heavily arabicized that a reader with no knowledge of Arabic meets with chronic difficulty in understanding it (Bayat, p. 34). Sheriar Irani would have found it hard to obtain many of these Arabic texts, though he would have understood that even high-ranking Shia Muslims inveterately had to be cautious in the expression of their philosophical convictions and wrote accordingly.

It was this background of vintage ishraqi "theosophy" (as it has sometimes been inadequately phrased in English) that rendered Sheriar at loggerheads with European and American Theosophy. At about the same time that he commenced his literary education, in 1885 Henry Olcott arrived in Bombay. Olcott had been one of the founders of the Theosophical Society in New York during the previous decade, and he enthusiastically created a Bombay branch which gained many Parsi and Hindu members. Olcott is well known for having expressed an esteem for Zoroastrianism, and was particularly keen on the *Desatir* (in English). But here any resemblance between he and Sheriar Irani ceased.

According to Olcott, the *Desatir* and the *Gathas* were equivalent to "occult science"; the mysteries of this science had been transmitted by Zarathushtra and his followers (the magi) "under the safe cover of an external ritual." To Olcott this meant that the Parsis should not abandon their rituals, but should instead preserve them diligently, while retrieving the lost key to the real meaning of these practices. To Sheriar this amounted to locking oneself in a prison and throwing away the key.

Sheriar had already learnt that it is difficult to persuade people to adopt a more enlightened view if they have already decided that they represent the ultimate. He was not a ritualist, having outgrown such adherence in his childhood. Anyone who has seriously studied the Kaivani background will know that the author, or authors, of the *Desatir* are most unlikely to have held a belief in the efficacy of ritual, not even as a "safe cover." They needed no such cover in an Islamic anti-ritualist milieu, and the *Desatir* does not express ritualistic views. With regard to the Gathas, it is now strongly arguable that Zarathushtra long predated the Median magi, and that he himself was a firm anti-ritualist to a marked degree, if not completely.

Later Western occult groupings of Europe and America are known to have adopted bizarre costume in the name of the belief that they were ritualistically perpetuating some arcane form of hierarchical expertise. Sheriar Irani would probably have been highly amused to see the photographs; being a genial man, he would probably have briefly remarked upon the desire for something fantastic in the otherwise drab lives of such people. He himself wore standard everyday clothing of his community, rather plain and inexpensive, and decidedly unobtrusive even in private company.

The "hidden masters" of Western Theosophy have been conflated with the prophets mentioned in the *Desatir* owing to Olcott's predilection for this much misunderstood treatise. Even the English translation of the *Desatir* does not say that the pre-Islamic prophets of the Mahabadian tradition became withdrawn from the world as the "hidden masters," though it does include the refrain that this tradition continually revives itself in the wake of the stifling ignorance of men. (See my Appendix in the present book).

To the mind of a Sheriar, the vintage Shia claim of "hidden" leaders made total sense in the context of such men as Hallaj and Sohravardi Maqtul being killed by authoritarian mandate when they were seen to be at variance with social and theocratic policies. Fancy having your tongue cut out? That is one of the reported indignities which Hallaj had to suffer in retribution for telling the authorities that there was something wrong with the exchequer and the local doctrine. This was a very far cry from an Olcott seeing "hidden masters" miraculously appearing before his privileged gaze with apparently nothing more remedial to communicate than the persistence of rituals.

It may have been the confrontation with Olcottian extravaganzas that made Sheriar even more determined to continue his Arabic and Persian researches. In any event, his mode of expression was very different to that of another Parsi contemporary who was averse to the proceedings of the Theosophical Society. This was Behramshah Novroji Shroff (d.1927), who was born at Bombay in 1858. Though Shroff was of priestly ancestry, like Sheriar he was reared in poverty and received very little education. Shroff did not in fact become a priest, but at the age of seventeen journeyed to Peshawar on India's North-West Frontier. From there he went to Iran, where he was allegedly led to Mount Demavand; here he gained enlightenment from "masters" who taught him the esoteric meaning of the Avesta. Afterwards he returned to India, where he settled at Surat and observed silence for nearly thirty years. If Sheriar had chanced to hear of him by this time, he might have been impressed, and hoped to find out more through the mists of rumour. But if so, then he would have tended to lose interest in 1902 when Shroff began to preach his esoteric version of the Avesta. Shroff was evidently influenced by the Kaivani heritage, but interpreted it in a rather diffuse manner. Much less in the Kaivani idiom was his insistence upon formal religious observance. Shroff gained a small but enthusiastic following in Surat and Bombay, and converted some Parsi priests at Udwada. His movement was not cosmopolitan but exclusively Zoroastrian, and became known as the Ilm-i Khshnum. It attempted to rival the Theosophical Society, but did not gain the same widespread allegiance among Parsis. Sheriar definitely knew of it in his later years, but did not become a member.

Sheriar Irani never claimed any dramatic esoteric experience. The most that he would ever mention, it seems, was his frightening experiences in prolonged meditation at the end of his dervishi. He never preached, beyond perhaps giving a fatherly sermon to his sons, or giving a friend or friends some advice. He respected the tenets of his native religion, but did not value its formalistic observance. He was not at all exclusive in his attitude to other traditions, and was sympathetic to many aspects of both the Islamic and Hindu heritages. He was not interested in rivalling any group or organization, even if he felt that they were in error. In this, he had a good example available to clear-headed study, due reflection, and action in life accordingly.

One factor that tends to stand out very strongly in the report of Azar Kaivan is his retiring disposition. Although he seems to have emigrated from Iran to India on account of the liberal climate of tolerance prevailing during Akbar's reign, he does not seem to have come into any physical contact with Akbar's court (though at his death some of his disciples are known to have settled at Agra, then known as

Akbarabad). Kaivan settled at Patna, a city well to the east of court affairs. There he continued to lead an austere contemplative existence, and shunned public admirers. The *Dabistan* says that he would not expose himself to any public limelight, and rarely consented to see anybody but his disciples and earnest seekers who wanted tuition. He is reported to have said that the majority of people are influenced by the conditioning of "time and place" against the cause of truth. He advised that the teachings prevalent amongst his group should be kept secret, and that each member should maintain the form of worship of their native religion. This double clause was a little more complex than it might seem, since he is on record as saying: "If you think properly, keep your tenets secret, concealing them even from your brethren in the faith, as they, for the confirmation of *their* system, will make you publicly known." (*Dabistan,* Shea-Troyer trans., Vol.1, p. 96, italics mine).

Kaivan's own immediate group of disciples appear to have been Zoroastrians. It is unlikely that Kaivan was warning them of the perils of persecution from the Parsis in India. It rather means that opponents would distort the concepts and methodology of his teaching while rebutting the rivalry they would deem it to constitute for them. Opponents would have no serious intention of attempting to understand such concepts, since such effort generally involves too much of a volte-face from more simplified ideology; where vested interests are concerned, such transition becomes impossible.

The cosmopolitan strain emerges very clearly amongst the pupils of Kaivan's disciples, with seven Muslims, two Jews, one Hindu brahmin, and one Portuguese Christian historically verifiable. But it is evident that there were other non-Zoroastrians connected personally with Kaivan during his lengthy residence in Patna, though any Muslim disciple is likely to have kept a low profile elsewhere, and even Hindus could be very resistant to foreign teachers in brahmanical circles. The close group of Zoroastrian disciples seem to have been largely composed of Iranis (and not Parsis), and hence may have overshadowed any other additional pupils in the oral tradition of the ensuing movement. Kaivan himself probably set very high standards for his pupils. That his outlook was liberal is attested by the *Dabistan* report that during his early years in Iran, he had decided upon a course of thorough acquaintance with the sciences of the philosophers of Greece, Iran, and India. These wise men of antiquity, it is added, transmitted to him all kinds of knowledge in a vision. The latter detail may well be a piece of literary embroidery, or rather an oral simplification of a fundamental experience of expanded consciousness such as is conceivable in the more acute philosophical training. It is apparent that Kaivan was a learned man, and the indications are that he was conversant with both Arabic and Persian, and quite possibly Indian languages also.

Sheriar Irani appears to have exemplified the practice of the Kaivani-*ishraqiyun* tradition in maintaining strict non-divulgence of personal achievements and related details, while tolerating the shortcomings of less perceptive individuals. Though he undoubtedly adhered to concepts that would have been considered (then as now) esoteric, his perspective appears to have been markedly at variance with more general vogues of the "esoteric" mentality. For instance, he believed in the capacity of rare human beings to be effective teachers in advanced experiential specifics, but he did not himself seek after the many teachers and mystical know-alls who were visible in his intercultural milieu. He participated in the more rare view which implies that such a teacher may not declare himself as one at all, in which case it would be practically impossible for all but the most perceptive individuals to recognize the genuine article. From this, it follows that it would be potential folly for anyone to assume such perceptive faculties. It also follows quite logically that the majority of those assuming such perception in themselves are easy fodder for bandwagon entrepreneurs.

If there is anything worse than superficial observers being accustomed to think that credentials must always be advertised, it must be those who assume that they would recognize such credentials even if they were kept "hidden."

Sheriar extended his linguistic achievements by learning to read and write Marathi, a vernacular dialect of Western India which put him in close touch with the Hindu population. Knowledge of the Hindu tradition was integral to the

Kaivani attitude, and though fluency in Marathi was not uncommon amongst Parsis, the ishraqi perspective was in general abeyance.

It was apparent to Sheriar that there were deficiencies not only in the more hidebound aspects of the Muslim and Hindu religions, but also in Zoroastrianism. But he did not adopt any shallow reformist outlook based on European ideas such as were very popular amongst nineteenth century Parsis. In his view, both the priestly conservativists and the westernized reformists were in error, though he would have conceded that the latter had more chance of discovering the truth – though not through the westernizing influences of lucre. While some of the orthodox diehards would not accept that only the Gathas could be taken as the actual words of Zarathushtra in the whole of the *Zend-Avesta* (a pertinent discovery of European scholars), the modernists were now apeing Western ways to such an extent that they were already promoting industrialism in Bombay, with some of them owning factories.

Available to educated Parsis of the late nineteenth century were Avestan and Pahlavi works in the original scripts, together with an Avestan grammar. Sheriar was inevitably interested in these developments, and must have delighted in researching ancient texts and correlating reformist lore with the education given him by his father Mundegar the *salar* at distant Kasimabad. But he was aware that his native tradition was incomplete in its mere textual and doctrinal idioms. Though he penned hymns in Gujarati for use by the Parsi community, more atypical was his poetry in Persian, which revealed more of his sufi background. He appears to have been a proficient poet in this language, and some of his *monajat* (mystical verses) were quoted in books of that day. He himself did not write books.

Though he was fluent in four languages, he did not learn English. He understandably did not have time to do everything, and possibly he found Westerners as puzzling as the British found the Hindus and Muslims. Ironically however, the Parsis and the British were ethnically closer to each other than to either Muslims or Hindus, a fact that is not without relish to the ethnographer.

People who knew Sheriar well had the strong impression that he remained a *dervish* at heart, despite his apparent involvement with mundane affairs. He might be said to have exemplified the sufi axiom: *"Dar dunya bash, az dunya mabash"* (Be in the world, but not of the world).

This particular axiom has sometimes been interpreted with a facile sense of convenience permitting excuses for not doing anything other than pursuing a materialistic career. In such usage, the axiom in reality amounts to: "Get the most out of the world while pretending to have transcended it." In Kaivani usage however, it was much more difficult to exploit the sentiment, since the standards of a *sirdasp* philosopher necessitated a firm anchorage in *hirtasp* ascetic principles. This was in consonance with the more rigorous forms of training attested in both Sunni and Shia dervish ranks, since the dervish lifestyle preceded an integration in mundane affairs. The dervish phase is necessarily lengthy and exacting, though opportunists invariably miss it out or modify it to the point of absurdity.

According to the Kaivani-irfani viewpoint, one cannot live properly in the world until one sees it in true perspective. It is those who approach life with an inadequate education (even if they are Ph.D's) and selfish ideas who distort its potential.

Some philanthropists have made good use of money and business concerns, while some standardized monastic orders have amassed large revenues for use in persecution programmes. It is clearly not the use of money that is necessarily wrong, but the attitude determining its use that is potentially abominable and despicable. The only way to correct wrong attitudes is to use a corrective which emerges in the behaviour pattern and the mindstream. The "contemplative approach" is something close to useless if it creates a false belief in one's detachment from the "worldly life" around one – rather similar perhaps to that of a Ph.D. in philosophy who never gets his feet wet and is unable to bang a nail successfully into a piece of wood. All ivory towers come crashing in the actual hour of revelation.

Sheriar had a good opportunity to discover how practical he was in the world owing to his marriage. Eight years after their atypical engagement, Sheriar and Shirin were married in 1892, when she was fourteen and he thirty-nine years of age. The union transpired to be a successful one.

A photograph taken not long after the wedding reveals Sheriar as a handsome man with long and drooping moustachios after the fashion of those days. Prevalent descriptions of his character and personality convey an impression of a calm disposition and a ready sense of humour. He possessed a robust constitution toughened by his mendicant travels, and though he no longer had to go hungry, he evinced a deep sympathy for those who did. Poona was a well-to-do city when compared with many slum areas of Bombay, but even in Poona there were beggars. Sheriar's own home was not luxurious by middle class Parsi standards; this small terraced dwelling was in the close vicinity of the British cantonment and could not boast any fine garden such as those he had formerly tended. This house was acquired at the time of his marriage from his hard-earned savings; his personal expenditure was very low, and hence he had accumulated capital and could no longer be classed as a poor man. He soon found that he had other mouths to feed, and expanded his business to include a toddy shop (some Parsi villages specialized in growing the toddy-palm, which was used for a drink that was low in alcoholic content).

Shirin did not possess the same range of experiences as her husband, but was in her later life described as a "queen among women," combining physical beauty with intelligence and wit. Like Sheriar she acquired a good command of languages, understanding four tongues altogether. She could speak Persian, but not Arabic.

The ex-labourer gained increased social respect as a business man, a writer, and as a virtual sage. People who would once have ignored him now felt pleased to pass the time of day with him. Hadn't he been just an illiterate gardener once, some kind of monk? But here he was so prosperous, so obviously knowledgeable, a social influence, with an intelligent wife whose beauty would last well into his old age.

As for the favoured man himself, now known as Sheriarji (the Hindu suffix *-ji* being a common designation of respect), he could not view many of his acquaintances with the same enthusiasm – though he did not make a point of emphasizing the disparity. Too many of them were stunted psychologies who had remained in the same response pattern they had formed in their youth, drugged by habitual thinking and petty objectives. Some were oppressed by their increasing age, gnawed by an uneasy sense of non-accomplishment which they continually tried to ignore or camouflage. Others were proud of themselves to the point of absurdity, as if the world could not exist without them.

Many of the other Parsi businessmen he knew did not regard money as a means to an end, but totally as the end in itself.

In addition to (or amongst) those who wanted "to get to know him," there must have been at least a few who preferred to think: "Was he not an ascetic once, a holy man? See, now he counts coins just like the rest of us." It is an observed fact of psychology that the jealous will often impute their own motives to someone else.

Sheriar had once tried to change his brother Khododad by a "holy" external lifestyle. He would not make the same error again.

This is not to say that Sheriar did not feel circumscribed by the horizons of his society. His unusual perspective on life was largely lost upon his family and relatives. His wife was clever to an extent well above average, and paid close heed to what he said, but his higher flights were lost upon her. He did not attempt to stress what could not effectively be heard, and instead matched himself to situational exigencies where a point of some consequence could be implemented at a time when someone was most receptive to it. It seems that one relative who was more than usually responsive to this was his brother-in-law Rustom (Masaji), who was also a tea shop proprietor but whose heart lay in the theatre. It was perhaps Rustom's sense of the dramatic which initially made him realize the extraordinary colour of Sheriar's life pattern. But drama is not necessarily concomitant with any full range of roles. Rustom did not pretend to understand Sheriar in his more revealing moods; he listened carefully however, and some of the content gradually became more clear to him.

The early twentieth century found Sheriar Irani the grey-haired father of five sons and one daughter.

It was not long before the First World War when he became aware of a distinctive new inhabitant of the cantonment area. An old woman had installed herself beneath a tree, a matriarch who lived exposed to all weathers just as he himself had once done. Yet he felt that this individual had gained a much deeper consciousness than he had ever accomplished. He had never seen anyone like her before, not during all his extensive travels. Like other onlookers, he at first asked himself: "Who is she? Where has she come from?"

He received a sense of shock to realize how old she was, that she had been grey-haired at the time of the Indian Mutiny. The deep wrinkles on her face amply substantiated the fragments of reminiscence that she occasionally divulged. Yet here was no senile face or composure; on the contrary, an extraordinarily vibrant dynamism hallmarked her speech and actions, even to a capacity for brisk walking. Her features he could locate as Afghan, slightly Mongoloid perhaps, a strongly boned visage with blue eyes typical of the Pathan. The combination of dynamism and compassion which she emanated told him other things also. She was already venerated in the vicinity as a holy person, and even the British had good cause to bear her in mind as a landmark. She gave an impression of something strangely untamed and yet completely natural, evincing a memorable sympathy and affinity with the poor. Her dynamism was extremely atypical for old women; even her luxuriant growth of white hair was distinctive.

Her method of speech seemed peculiarly fitting for the intercultural focus that she became in Poona; it was almost unintelligible to casual hearing (the British were puzzled by her statements), a mixture of different languages which mingled highly abstract references with aphorisms of a more obvious wisdom. There was no doctrine conveyed, not the slightest attempt at persuasion to any dogma or teaching. But personal instructions she did give on occasion.

Who was she? She came to be known as Hazrat Babajan, but this was a vestigial identity. Her history was subsequently pieced together, bit by bit, but Sheriar Irani knew more about her from personal contact than any potted history could tell him. He would not have said that he believed her to be a Completed Human (*insan-i-kamil*); she existed independently of belief, independently of her hundreds of admirers, devotees, and disciples.

Sheriar had by now become intimately conversant with obscure texts whose titles could not even be pronounced properly by his compatriots. He was himself a source of *irfani* and related lore to anyone who could tap it, but he felt very small in relation to Babajan.

He had the advantage over many Hindus and Zoroastrians who converged upon her, since she spoke a good deal in Persian and Arabic. Yet there was no religious insularity in her approach, and though evidently born a Sunni Muslim, she did not discriminate in the least against adherents of other religions. Nor was there a single trace of the "sufi order" mentality; she declared no *tariqat* or *silsila*, though she did indicate that she had long ago known teachers in more northern areas of India.

It seems that in his own earlier days Sheriar Irani had sought hard for a teacher, but found all potential entities for this role as either inaccessible, of partial qualification only, or downright frauds. In a world full of counterfeits he had deemed it best to remain an *uwaysi,* tending to give the impression of a Kaivani bibliophile to literate Parsis. Now he felt that he knew in more depth about the sentiment expressed in the old sufi adage that the enlightened ones will not forget you, even though you forget them, providing that you have remained true to the cause they serve.

According to Kaivani tradition, important events of developmental value are dependent upon influences facilitating a supercession of the psycho-conditioning of "time and place" which constricts the manifestation of truth among the majority of humans. The minority who evade this conditioning are often dubbed the elect according to various terminologies, but in actuality such evasion can occur inversely, creating bizarre mutations who delight in their "elect" sense of status and weird tangent which is not infrequently a short cut to insanity.

Our ex-dervish was keenly aware of such anomalies and had always taken care to steer his way past exploiters. Babajan was not an exploiter; any money given to her was redistributed amongst the poor, and her own comforts were negligible in the extreme. Sheriar now led a comfortable life as a moderately prosperous businessman and was able to change his former small residence for a larger one in the same vicinity of unostentatious dwellings. If ever he conceived himself as one of the elect, there is no record of his having done so.

It seems apt enough to observe, however, that he had searched for someone answering to the atypical charisma of this matriarch over many thousands of miles, and had finally thought never to see a day of fulfillment in this respect; with his inveterate sense of humour, he probably had several mature smiles over the irony that the matriarch came to him, almost on his doorstep, in the same cantonment purlieus.

In the Kaivani perspective, the right efforts will eventually bring their full reward, even if not immediately, and this reward is not necessarily to be conceived in any material sense, as many do in effect conceive of the end product.

In his childhood Sheriar had spent much of his time on a desolate hill tending corpses. Then he had become a dervish in two sprawling countries; subsequently he had become a manual labourer, and afterwards a self-taught scholar, finally to become a successful business and family man. Yet this was not the ultimate stage in his vocation, one in which he did not lose his presence of mind.

In view of his increasing infirmity during his old age, he acquired a business partner, a young man whose identity has survived as M. This partner looked after the shop duties, while Sheriar attended to the auctions specializing in toddy tree lots. In the course of time he handed over this aspect of affairs likewise to M, and finally all that was required of him was his signature. One evening M invited him to dinner, and after a pleasant meal and conversation, casually passed him another business document to sign, explaining that it merely concerned another toddy lot deal. Sheriar quickly obliged.

He was afterwards informed that this document represented him as handing over his share of the business as an unconditional gift to M. The unscrupulous young partner quickly put in his claim, and the issue went before the courts. Owing to her husband's ill-health, Shirin had to cope with the brunt of legal matters involved, and could not understand Sheriar's view of the matter. He would say that they (he and his wife) were not the losers, but that M would lose. M would inevitably have to work out his error in future lives, which would entail suffering in accordance with the laws of cause and effect which none escaped. In this context, Sheriar would also quote the sufi adage that "the laws of God are finer than the hairs of the head."

Shirin's response to these disclosures was to say that such retribution was of no practical use now. She would be dead by then, and she would not even recognize M in her next life. They had lost the business, and the money and jewellery stored in their bank account would all be lost in court expenses – and would not benefit their children.

Sheriar has accordingly been represented by some as a gullible old man who had too much faith in the goodness of his fellow humans.

There is another side to the episode. For some thirty and more years, Sheriar had conducted himself in an exemplary fashion according to middle class notions of "getting on in the world." He had procured well for his family, and was fully aware of the value of his assets in the bank. He also knew that the trouble with poor people becoming richer is that they always want more, and tend to end up like the affluent who do nothing of value, consumed only with the desire to accumulate further assets.

From what I have learnt of Sheriar Irani, he was quite capable of giving all his relatives an object lesson in the flux of vanities. His own assets were quite sufficient to defray court expenses, and most of his sons were now adult and able to demonstrate viable livelihood capacities. He owned his house. More to the point perhaps, he himself preferred a simple life, and he was nearly at the end of his days.

Sheriar's "second renunciation" can be viewed as an ace card in demonstrating to those Parsis who had not yet become completely Westernized that he at least was not in need of all the securities of high wealth and its attendant anxieties and evils, and that the true dervish always remains one despite changes in career adaptation and projection.

At the age of seventy (it was now the 1920's) Sheriar would go to the law court with the name of *Yazdan* on his lips – this being a Zoroastrian term for deity, favoured in the *Desatir* amongst other sources. This veteran Yazdani felt that a cycle of experience was repeating itself on a higher spiral, that he was going forward once again into the unknown, though with increasingly open eyes – he was again setting out from restriction upon the journey that breaks all horizons.

The judge finally stated that Sheriar had been deceived, but the fact remained that he had signed the document; by a strangely illogical process in terms of explicit values, the court therefore ruled in M's favour.

The preference for paperwork as opposed to the truth did not altogether surprise Sheriar; he probably felt glad to be no longer a proprietor of a toddy establishment, since he himself had been a teetotaller all his life.

When the case was over, he sent a message to M, saying that he forgave him – though adding that some day M might want to ask his forgiveness and he would doubtless be dead by then, and so it was a matter between M and God.

When M was himself an old man and helplessly bedridden, he experienced acute remorse for his underhand ruse. But by then it was too late to make amends, since by then both Sheriar and his wife were deceased.

The last years of Sheriar Irani were relatively contemplative; yet he would have said that his life had always been fundamentally contemplative, ever since his childhood on the hilltop at Kasimabad. He wondered at people who were not reflective – did they not realize that being unable to stop the momentum of their daily flow of impressions, that they rushed headlong into whatever trap circumstances contrived, into any situational shock, into any environmental upset – with no insulation save devices for putting awareness into oblivion?

This angle of vantage rendered him somewhat ahead of the customary insulation between businessmen and scholars such as tends to be current in today's world, e.g., scholars tend to regard all businessmen as rank opportunists, while businessmen tend to regard all scholars as impractically obscurantist. Sheriar himself, as a businessman-cum-savant, knew that both roles were limited in different ways, though his own penchant was more in alignment with scholarly topics than mercantile ones.

It is interesting to compare Sheriar's role with that of Maneckji Dhalla, the Parsi high priest of Karachi. As a young man, the latter had been sent to New York to gain a university grounding in Iranist studies. He went as a priest, and returned as a Ph.D. Despite Dhalla's reformist condemnation of ritual however, in many ways he remained a conservative theologian. Yet Sheriar would probably have considered it more apt for Dhalla to have accepted what Boyce calls a "modern Western version of the old Zurvanite heresy" (Boyce, p. 213) than to have outrightly rejected the validity of Kaivani ideas and experiences. Amongst the accusations levelled by Dhalla against the Kaivanis was that many of them found consolation in the teachings of Hindu yogis. According to Dhalla's version of the *Dabistan,* Hirbed the Parsi mystic told his pupil Mobad Hushiyar to burn or bury his body when dead (Hirbed was actually an Irani philosopher, and there is no proof that Hushiyar was his pupil), while the *Desatir* states that it matters not whether a corpse is consigned to the fire or to the earth. Dhalla was evidently outraged that Kaivani philosophers and mystics could so ignore traditional burial practices; some people's views are beyond belief.

Dhalla did not like the *Dabistan*, finding its statements uncorroborated by the writings of Zoroastrian priests. He seems to have been offended that the *Dabistan* mentions a Parsi ascetic who travelled through Gujerat garbed like a

Hindu renunciate and who visited the Sikh Guru Har Govind. It seems that even a Ph.D. did not confer upon a high priest the capacity to praise those individuals who transcended the ethnocentric and ideocentric ruts imposed by class-conscious sacerdotalists of all kinds.

Dhalla was one of those who confused Western Theosophy with Kaivani teachings (the reason being that since both were contrary to conservative doctrine, they were lumped together by detractors whose sense of scholarship is not particularly stunning). He found it unpalatable that the *Dabistan* asserted that Zarathushtra had couched his teachings in figurative and enigmatic language. Dhalla concluded that the Kaivani teachings in the *Dabistan* were based upon earlier sufi teachings and developed under Hindu mystical influences. He found it unconducive to his taste that certain Kaivani ascetic practices mentioned in the *Dabistan* were reminiscent of yogic feats, e.g., standing on the head from nightfall to sunrise (which someone like Sheriar might have informed him was also compatible with the sufi symbolism of being upside down in relation to the false world). More fabulous to the incredulous Dhalla were the reports of Kaivani "powers", e.g., reading the thoughts of others, detaching from the physical body at will, rendering oneself invisible to men, and bringing the dead to life. Such reports were interpreted literally by Dhalla, and perhaps even by the compiler of the *Dabistan*; Sheriar might have interposed that although it was possible to render a dervish invisible as a businessman, it was extremely difficult to resuscitate some "dead" high priests and other Parsis bent on technological prowess and streamlined factories.

Dhalla expressed the view that the Kaivani "theosophy" was in direct antagonism to the "worldly spirit" of the Zoroastrian faith (Dhalla, p. 469). Sheriar would have concurred, but from a diametrically opposite perspective.

Less objectionable in Sheriar's view were the attempts of Ibrahim Pur-Davud to portray Zoroastrian history. The latter scholar was of Muslim parentage, and was prominent in the reevaluation of the non-Islamic Iranian heritage which was a feature attendant upon the installation of the new Pahlavi dynasty in Iran during the 1920's. Pur-Davud was highly sympathetic to Zoroastrianism, and made the *Avesta* accessible to Muslim Iranians in Persian translation. His version of the Gathas was translated into English and published in Bombay during the late 1920's; Sheriar would not have been able to read the English, but would have been at no disadvantage with the Persian. Parsis were appreciative of Pur-Davud's efforts, and the more educated and liberal Muslims in Iran were enabled to feel a greater respect for pre-Islamic events in their country. Boyce says that in basing his work on the contributions of European scholars, Pur-Davud modified the implications of the dualism between good and evil (Boyce, p. 220) – a philosophical dualism of which Pur-Davud actually approved highly. A man like Sheriar would have seen no need to modify the philosophical dualism – which is somewhat different in aspect to the theological – and could have pointed out that there were evils in both modernism and conservatism alike.

Some Shia scholars have expressed an interest in the subject of Azar Kaivan, but seem deterred by the implications of pancultural ramifications. This is perhaps a great pity, because the Kaivani phenomenon may well hold an important key to the essential Islamic tradition just as it may also hold the key to Iran's more antique history.

Sheriar's view of the Sunni versus Shia conflict was that of all Kaivanis – it cannot be blamed on the Prophet Muhammad. As a member of a persecuted minority faction, he remained faithful to that minority from his Kaivani perspective. As the underdog to first Shia Muslims and then the Christian British, he may well have deemed that the only philosophy which could remedy all ills was one outside all cast-iron ideology. That may be why he found it so difficult to communicate with so many convinced and vehement people.

The British were very proud of their Graeco-Roman heritage, and regarded this as something setting them apart from other races. It is pertinent to reflect that if Sheriar had known much of Greek philosophy in its Islamic guise as mediated by the ishraqi tradition, he would never have been able to convince his Indo-European overlords (not even by using the King's best English) that his own tradition knew as much, or even more, about the essential Greeks than Gibbon and other latter day sages.

In his own community, divulgence of his views would have tagged him as unpatriotically unorthodox even by such avant garde dasturs as Dhalla. There would have been no drastic punishment for his heretical views, but he was one of those who felt that the pursuit of argument is useless when the opponents have no intention of changing their minds even in the event of being proven wrong.

Sheriar Mundegar Irani died virtually an octogenarian in April 1932, only six months following the decease of the matriarch who dwelt beneath the nearby *neem* tree in the Poona cantonment area. By that time, he had long been able to look detachedly upon the way in which he had nearly killed himself in meditation in a remote jungle, and could better appreciate deeper incentives attendant upon birth as an illiterate member of an oppressed minority.

Sociological conclusion:

On the strong indications that I have researched, the subject was an effective successor to the best philosophical tradition in his native community, a tradition which he actually outgrew in respect of certain adjuncts imposed by cultural trends of expression. The subject affords an example of the code of reticence that tends to characterize persecuted minorities, and which is fully explicable. There is also a specimen of transition from a wandering, illiterate lifestyle to a sedentary literate lifestyle synchronous with the increasing adaptive changes of two related minority groupings in different countries and under different sociocultural stresses.

BIBLIOGRAPHY

For Zarathushtra and some aspects of *batini* history, see my *Minds and Sociocultures: Variations and Transitions* (forthcoming), Part Two and Appendix. For an extension on Zarathushtra's dating, see Appendix Four of my *Ancient Cultures in Flux* (forthcoming). For an orthodox treatment of Zarathushtra and the Zoroastrian tradition, see M. Boyce, *Zoroastrians: Their Religious Beliefs and Practices* (London: Routledge & Kegan

Paul, 1979). For another treatment of the early Islamic conquests, see P.K. Hitti, *History of the Arabs* (tenth edn, London: Macmillan, 1970). For a treatment of Salman Farsi, see S.H. Nasr in *The Cambridge History of Iran Vol. 4* (Cambridge University Press, 1975), pp. 446–7. The material available on Bayazid Bistami is scholastically debateable in certain respects, but his Zoroastrian background is not in question. A.J. Arberry's trans. of Attar's version of Bayazid in *Muslim Saints and Mystics* (London: Routledge & Kegan Paul, 1966), pp. 100 ff., presents a Sunni portrait of the subject expressed at least three centuries after the event. The standard work on Hallaj is Louis Massignon's *La Passion de Husayn Ibn Mansur Hallaj* (second edn, Paris: Gallimard, 1975, 4 vols); trans. by H. Mason as *The Passion of Hallaj*, 4 vols (Princeton University Press, 1982). Massignon's magnus opus entailed intensive research eclipsing many former views, and seems to have been seldom read in its French original. On Junayd, see the sympathetic treatment of A.H. Abdel-Kader, *The Life, Personality and Writings of Al-Junayd* (London: Luzac, 1962). Sources relating to Sohravardi Maqtul are only partially represented in European languages, though helpful is Henry Corbin's *Suhrawardi d'Alep fondateur de la doctrine illuminative* (Paris: Maisonneuve, 1939). The same scholar's *En Islam Iranien, Tome II: Sohrawardi et les Platoniciens de Perse* (Paris: Gallimard, 1971), though indisputably extensively familiar with manuscript sources, goes surprisingly little further forward in the delineation of ishraqi methods and objectives.

For a detailed modern investigation of the Yazd environment in sympathy with traditionalist ideas, see M. Boyce, *A Persian Stronghold of Zoroastrianism* (Oxford: Clarendon Press, 1977). The report of A.V. Williams Jackson is contained in his *Persia Past and Present: A Book of Travel and Research* (New York: Macmillan, 1906), pp. 353 ff. The report of E.G. Browne is to be found in his *A Year Amongst the Persians* (London: Adam and Charles Black, 1893; third edn, Cambridge University Press, 1950, pp. 403 ff.). For Browne's account of the Bab, see *ibid.*, pp. 64 ff. On the *lutigars* see W.M. Floor, "The Lutis – A Social Phenomenon in Qajar Persia," *Die Welt des Islams* (Leiden 1971) 13: 102–120.

Relevant to the Babi phenomenon is F. Kazeni, "Some Preliminary Observations on the Early Development of Babism,"

Muslim World (1973) 63: 119–131. See also E.G. Browne, ed. and trans., *A Traveller's Narrative written to illustrate the Episode of the Bab* (two vols, Cambridge University Press, 1891). This is an anonymous work probably written in 1886, and is fundamentally a Bahai text. In his introduction, Browne reports that the Bab explicitly and repeatedly declared in all his works that the religion he established and the books revealed to him were in no way final (Vol.2, p. xvii). See also E.G. Browne, trans., *The Tarikh-i-Jadid or New History of Mirza Ali Mhd the Bab* (Cambridge University Press, 1893), which is more original, though still a reworking of an earlier Babi text. On the Babis, see also H. Algar, *Religion and State in Iran 1785–1906: The Role of the Ulama in the Qajar Period* (Berkeley: University of California Press, 1969), pp. 137 ff., remarking of the Bab's confinements that the degree of his contact with followers seems uncertain, though such contact was not totally curtailed. See also M. Bayat, *Mysticism and Dissent: Socioreligious Thought in Qajar Iran* (New York: Syracuse University Press, 1982), pp. 87 ff., observing that distortions and selective omissions of facts and ideas are evident in accounts written after the Bab's death by followers of the two rival contenders for his succession, meaning the Azalis and Bahais. The court historian Lisan al-Mulk found it convenient to depict the Bab as a mentally deranged sufi. Bayat says that the Bab early had a Shaikhi teacher, and that the influence of Shaikhi ideas is clearly discernible in the Bab's works.

For Muhammad al-Murtada's report on the Ghazali brothers, see J. Spencer Trimingham, *The Sufi Orders in Islam* (Oxford: Clarendon Press, 1971), p. 33. Trimingham includes a very brief report on the Gunabadis (*ibid.*, pp. 101–2) which largely amounts to a quote from the Russian scholar W. Ivanow. Cf. N. Pourjavady and P.L. Wilson, *Kings of Love: The Poetry and History of the Ni'matullahi Sufi Order* (Tehran: Imperial Iranian Academy of Philosophy, 1978). For Bernard Carra De Vaux on "Tanasukh", see *The Encyclopaedia of Islam* (first edn., Leiden: E.J. Brill), Vol. 4, pp. 648–9.

For Rypka on Haji Sabzavari, see J. Rypka *et al, A History of Iranian Literature* (Dordrecht: Reidel, 1968), pp. 343–4, citing Y.E. Bertels, *Ocherk istorii persidskoy literaturi* (1928). E.G. Browne's early and valuable account of Sabzavari can be found in *A Year Amongst the Persians,* pp. 143 ff. Also helpful is

S.H. Nasr, "Haji Mulla Hadi Sabziwari" (1543–56) in M.M. Sharif, ed., *A History of Muslim Philosophy Vol. 2* (Wiesbaden: Otto Harrassowitz, 1966).

The life of Sheriar Irani would not have been possible to write without personal contact with the subject's family; I am indebted to Sheriar's son Adi S. Irani for certain background data. An article by another of Sheriar's sons, Jal S. Irani, appeared in *Divya Vani* (Hyderabad, Andhra Pradesh, 1965, ed. Swami Satya Prakash Udaseen); this relates basic events in Sheriar's life, and reveals the curiously pronounced gulf between conventional assessment and deeper implications. A useful and informative article on Sheriar's background in Yazd was supplied by N. Anzar in *The Glow* (Dehra Dun, 1976) 11(3): 3–10. The episode concerning the termination of Sheriar's business activities has appeared in a variant in N. Anzar, *The Beloved: The Life and Work of Meher Baba* (North Myrtle Beach, S.C.: Sheriar Press Inc., 1974), pp. 4–5, but as I understand it, the report is incomplete. An early account of Sheriar Irani appeared in C.B. Purdom, *The Perfect Master* (London: Williams & Norgate, 1937), pp. 14–16, but is disappointingly brief and contains at least two factual errors.

For an account of Parsi activity in India, see E. Kulke, *The Parsees in India: A Minority as Agent of Social Change* (Munchen: Weltforum Verlag, 1974). For a good account of Akbarian India, see S.A.A. Rizvi, *Religious and Intellectual History of the Muslims in Akbar's Reign* (New Delhi: Munshiram Manoharlal, 1975). On Swamis Vivekananda and Sadananda, see Sister Christine's reliable account in *Reminiscences of Swami Vivekananda by his Eastern and Western admirers* (Calcutta: Advaita Ashrama, 1961), pp. 190 ff., 204 ff. For Vivekandanda and Ingersoll, see *The Life of Swami Vivekananda by his Eastern and Western Disciples* (fourth edn, Calcutta: Advaita Ashrama, 1949), pp. 327–8. On the Turkomans, see B. Spuler, "Central Asia from the Sixteenth Century to the Russian Conquests" (468–494) in *The Cambridge History of Islam Vol. 1* (Cambridge University Press, 1970), and partic. p. 482 for slaves, religious classes, and khanates.

A translation of the *Dabistan* exists in mid-nineteenth century English, and is unreliable in many places: see D. Shea and A. Troyer, trans., *The Dabistan or School of Manners,* 3 vols (Paris: Oriental Translation Fund of Great Britain and Ireland,

1843). An abridged version has recently appeared as *The Religion of the Sufis* (London: Octagon Press 1979), but this contains only the section on the sufis of Islam. The entry from *The Encyclopaedia of Islam* (new edn, Leiden: E.J. Brill), Vol. 2 (1965) is "Dabistan al-Madhahib" by J. Horovitz – H. Masse, and the attribution of authorship is acceptable by many scholars. Still an important source of information is an article by Jivanji J. Modi, one of the most learned scholars that the Parsis produced this century: "A Parsee High Priest (Dastur Azar Kaiwan, 1529–1614 A.D.) with his Zoroastrian disciples in Patna, in the 16th and 17th Century A.C.," *Jnl of the K.R. Cama Oriental Institute* (Bombay 1932), 20: 1–85. Modi not only revised the accepted dating here, but pointed out that there is no evidence in the *Dabistan* that Azar Kaivan was a Dastur (high priest); Modi himself was a hereditary priest of a fire temple. Far less sympathetic to the subject was the brief account of M.N. Dhalla in his *History of Zoroastrianism* (New York: Oxford University Press, 1938), pp. 464 ff. Dastur Dhalla really was a Parsi high priest, and maintained both priestly and academic credentials. Cf. the more favourable reference by Seyyed Hossein Nasr in M.M. Sharif, ed., *A History of Muslim Philosophy Vol. 1* (Wiesbaden, 1963), p. 397 note 73. At the end of his article on Sohravardi Maqtul, Nasr inserts that Corbin and other European scholars have stressed the role of ishraqi wisdom in the Kaivani tradition; Nasr calls the Kaivani movement an eclectic one in which elements of Hinduism, Buddhism, Islam and Zoroastrianism are combined, and which was similar to the liberal trends at the Mughal court of Akbar. Nasr points out that the Kaivanis paid marked attention to the writings of Sohravardi Maqtul, and reiterates that Kaivan's disciple Farzaneh Behram ibn Farshad translated several works of Maqtul into Persian. Nasr also comments that the Kaivani movement left in its wake several works like the *Desatir*.

The late Professor Henry Corbin, one of the leading European scholars of Iranian religious and philosophical literature, gave a few pages to the Kaivani school in his *En Islam Iranien,* Vol. 2, pp. 354 ff. Corbin evidently regarded the *Desatir* as a product of the Kaivani tradition. He pointed out that the *Desatir* has certain parallels with a voluminous work of Farzaneh Behram ibn Farhad entitled *Sharistan-i chahar chaman*; this Persian treatise describes a sequence of Iranian prophets, in addition to cosmographic and other details. Corbin emphasizes that this work of Kaivan's disciple has ishraqi themes in its composition. The *Sharistan* was published in Bombay in 1862–3 by Zoroastrians.

The *Desatir* was "carefully published by Mulla Firuz Bin Kaus" to quote from the title page again. This two-volume edition (Bombay 1818) included a glossary of the "obsolete and technical Persian terms" by Mulla Firuz, and the English translation gives a passable idea of the contents. The editorial preface by Mulla Firuz acknowledged the assistance of the British scholar William Erskine; the catalogue of the Cambridge University Library states that the translation is by Erskine. Mulla Firuz was evidently aided by numerous British subscribers and a couple of British assistants, imparting to this undertaking a distinct flavour of Anglo-Parsi goodwill relations. According to J.J. Modi (*art. cit.*, pp. 15–16), the English translation of the *Desatir* was made, with the help of Mulla Firuz, by William Erskine, who was then acting as Chief Police Officer of Bombay, and who had been requested to undertake his literary task by Sir John Malcolm, then Governor of Bombay.

For Erskine's interpretation of the *Desatir* and *Dabistan,* see Appendix Two of the present work. For further information on the background of these two Persian treatises, see my *The Resurrection of Philosophy,* chapters eight and nine.

For a biography of Babajan, see my *A Sufi Matriarch: Hazrat Babajan* (Cambridge: Anthropographia Publications, 1986).

PART TWO:

THE KAIVANI-ISHRAQI GROUPS OF MUGHAL INDIA

Some confusion has existed about many of the features attendant upon the introduction of the Kaivani phenomenon into India from Iran, and its subsequent existence and projection. The *Dabistan* is the chief source of information, but is not always as clear as modern historians would wish, though that work has been very largely neglected despite its singularly catholic sense of universalism and intercultural reporting. In addition, there exist not a few supplementary sources of information which are not always perceived for what they are and consequently remain unintegrated in the study of the history of thought.

The Parsi scholar Modi early pointed out that the *Dabistan* relates how the Mughal emperor Akbar (rgd. 1556–1605) wrote letters to Azar Kaivan in Iran and invited him to India.[1] Modi was debating who it was that influenced Akbar's integration of Zoroastrian elements in his famous universalist policy of *sulh-i kul* or "peace with all," a policy that lent to his reign an almost unparalleled sense of tolerance and religio-philosophical latitude in which sages, scientists and scholars of different religions and sects met in free speech debates and conferences, and in which the Hindu population was viewed as a religio-cultural entity in its own right, and not merely as a strategic ally, and not as a rival or foe.

By 1582–4 Akbar had openly adopted some of the Parsi forms of worship. For some ten years the monarch had been on good terms with the Parsi inhabitants of India, and a few years earlier Dastur Meherji Rana of Navsari had been invited to a discussion held at the Mughal court between the representatives of various religions. Akbar had gained a favourable impression of Zoroastrianism and wanted to learn the terminology of that religion. He even adopted an ancient custom reported of the Persian kings, and kept a sacred fire perpetually burning at his court both night and day. The monarch is known to have conferred the Islamic title of *mulla* upon at least two Parsi priests in deference to their religious learning, and even requested the Safavid monarch Shah Abbas I to send him a learned Zoroastrian from Iran to help in compiling a Persian dictionary, with the result that Dastur Ardeshir Nushirvan of Kirman sojourned at Akbar's court in 1597.[2]

Yet there exists a vacuum of information about the participation of Azar Kaivan in the cultural life of that era. The date when this leader of the Yazdanian and (Maha)Abadian groups (as the *Dabistan* refers to him) emigrated to India is lacking, but it appears to have been well before the end of the sixteenth century. The fact that he was not an orthodox priest (and possibly not even a priest at all, not even by birth) might account for his comparative oblivion in this respect. If Akbar wanted a man like this at his court, he would have found it difficult to achieve, since philosophers like Kaivan maintained the practice of keeping "far from the crowd." Though Kaivan would have respected the monarch's latitude, he would not have been greatly interested in debate or discussion. His attitude was already liberal, and he conceivably thought that it was necessary for orthodox theologians of various persuasions to educate themselves a little more before any greater educational influx could occur. His perspective was, for instance, radically different to that of the Parsi priesthood, who would probably have viewed him as an alien.

It is evident that Akbar himself was not unduly impressed by some of the views and attitudes with which he was confronted in his cosmopolitan milieu. He was careful to listen to everyone, and would personally participate in discussions with learned men who came to his court from various countries. But the preaching of the Jesuit missionaries did not convert him; the Shia *ulama* did not win him over, though he found them refined by comparison with the Sunni *ulama* of India, some of whom harboured a resentment of his policy. One of those whom Akbar did esteem was the sufi shaikh Tajuddin, who represented the philosophy known as *wahdat al-wujud,* an encounter which as Mujeeb comments, must have afforded Akbar an indication of the depth inherent in the more esoteric form of Islam. The monarch and his advisers were particularly averse to the stigmatization of Hindus, and amongst the measures taken in this respect was to reduce the eating of meat and to prohibit cow-sacrifice amongst Muslims in an attempt to narrow the gulf in customs that existed between Hindus and Muslims. Yet Akbar also wanted to abolish the anomalous Hindu custom of *suttee*, but was ironically unable to do so for fear of offending Hindu sentiments, though he did ensure that it was publicized that no woman need follow her husband to the funeral pyre if she did not want to.[3]

It emerges that Akbar wished to meet enlightened representatives of traditional thinking, but found them a distinct minority. It was the missionaries and adventurers who tended to throng to his court; those less inclined to persuasion were more difficult to enlist. Some of those sufi types who exemplified the monistic-pantheistic teaching of *wahdat al-wujud* (whether professedly or no) adopted a lifestyle of comparative seclusion, partly in retreat from the intrigues of courtiers and theologians.

Modi aptly inferred that it was not Parsi orthodoxy which drew Kaivan and his group to India, but the liberal aspects of Akbar's policy. Kaivan did not reside close to the Mughal court, but instead settled at Patna in Bihar. The reason for his selection of this North Indian city is not clear, though it is unlikely to have been owing to the fact that it was an old Buddhist centre. The only Buddhists left in India were now very largely the pilgrims from other countries, notably Tibet. (Many Buddhist ideas were not foreign to Kaivanis, though the actual emphases were different in the respective Yazdanian and Lamaist camps). Though Akbar gained interviews with brahmins, yogis, Jaina ascetics, Portuguese Christian fathers, sufi *pirs*, and Parsi *dasturs* and *mobads*, there is no recorded mention of any such interview with Azar Kaivan. Some of the latter's disciples are reported to have gone to Agra after his death, and it would be extremely tenuous to infer from this that Kaivan delegated representatives to the court.

Modi inferred that the date of Kaivan's arrival in India was *circa* 1581–5, and stressed that it was later nineteenth century writers who affirmed that the subject was a Dastur or high priest. There is no such evidence in the *Dabistan* for this sacerdotal status. Modi also considered it a confusion that Kaivan was later thought to have had a son, a confusion owing to a similarity of names. Modi even differed with B.B. Patel on the date of Kaivan's death, owing to the margin afforded by discrepancies in manuscripts. Patel had accepted the date of 1614 for the decease, but Modi opted for 1618, which takes us further into the reign of Jehangir. Since Kaivan is reported to have died at the age of eighty-five, Modi fixed his date of birth at 1533.[4]

If Modi is correct, then Kaivan was a veteran in Yazdanian-ishraqi philosophy by the time he settled in Patna.[5] In all probability he had no priestly background at all, or at least was not a practising priest. His was an ascetic existence, but his aloofness from the court does not preclude an influence upon its policy, however indirect the contribution may have been (and which is most unlikely to have involved a literal sacred fire).

One of the intermediaries between the court and Azar Kaivan could have been none other than Bahauddin Amili (1547–1621), also known in Iran as Shaikh-i-Bahai. The author of the *Dabistan* states that he had heard from Farzaneh Behram ibn Farshad that one day Amili, the *mujtahid* of the Shi'is, had gained an interview with Kaivan, and thereafter become his diligent pupil and mixed with his circle. This reference is important, since apart from its significance in terms of a Muslim appendage to the circle of Zoroastrian ishraqis, Amili was a very eminent entity in Safavid society. Born at Baalbek in Syria, he had emigrated to Iran at the age of thirteen with his Shi'i father; his scholarly capacity was high, and he eventually became the *Shaikh al-Islam* of the capital at Isfahan. Yet despite this eminence as a theological authority, and despite his proximity to the court of Shah Abbas I, some of his writings reveal sufi inclinations and he has accordingly gained the reputation of a sufi. Amili is a complex figure because he was a *mujtahid* who was still working according to the old polymath tradition of medieval Iran, and was an outstanding scientist for his time. This polymath tradition can be very favourably compared to that of the European Renaissance, though it was to increasingly stagnate and die out in Iran during the seventeenth century in the shadow of the increasing authority devolving upon the new Shi'ite hierocracy. Nearly ninety books have been attributed to Amili's pen, but it is not necessary to defer to all of these in order to recognize his intellectual abilities. Nasr observes that Amili revived the study of mathematics and astronomy in Iran after these subjects had suffered a century of neglect, producing a treatise on algebra and several on astronomy. He was also the leading Safavid architect, planning the Shah mosque of Isfahan. He also found time to be one of the most competent Safavid poets, writing *mathnavis* which display a flair for witty anecdote in the sufi-inspired tradition of Rumi and others. He spent many of his mature years travelling with dervishes and visiting various entities of sufi repute. As a consequence of his diverse roles, he was respected alike by theologians, philosophers, and sufis (between whom the dividing lines were often pronounced), to the extent that each of these factions considered him as one of their own.[6]

It was certainly not every scientist who could have bridged the gap between *qalandars* and court *ulama*. It is not known what year Amili came to Azar Kaivan's abode, but it could have been before the end of Akbar's reign; the same can be said of one of Amili's associates, namely Mir Abu'l Qasim Findiriski (d.1640). The latter was not a theologian, but a philosopher. He had some knowledge of medicine and mathematics in his role as a teacher of the *Shifa* and *Qanun* of Ibn Sina (Avicenna) at Isfahan. The Safavid capital know Findiriski as a Peripatetic philosopher, but he also travelled widely in India and acquired a sufi reputation. His affinity with liberal attitudes is attested by the two works he wrote on the *Yoga Vashishta,* a Hindu work that was available in a Persian translation. He actually appears to have spent more time in India than in Persia, and in the Mughal realm was respected by many princes and personally knew a large number of Hindu sages and yogis.

Findiriski's latitude makes it easy to understand why he appeared in the pages of the *Dabistan,* where he is described as gaining the company of Azar Kaivan's disciples, as a consequence of which he became an adherent of *ahimsa* principles and a "worshipper of the sun."[7] Bahauddin Amili is also referred to in the context of Kaivan's circle, but evidently also met Kaivan himself, and therefore Findiriski may well have been a personal associate of the Patna ishraqi, retaining an identity in Kaivan's circle after his death. The *ahimsa* principles were not strange to liberal Muslims of that era owing to the Akbarian policy, and these principles would have afforded a felicitous meeting-point between Hindus, Muslims, and Kaivani Zoroastrians. In this context it is of added significance that the *Dabistan* relates that when Findiriski was asked why he did not go on pilgrimage to Mecca, he replied that he preferred not to go because prevalent customs meant that he would have to slaughter a sheep with his own hands. Interestingly, such an explicit anti-ritual attitude would have clearly separated the Kaivanis from Parsi practices, since the Parsi priests still maintained the sacrifice of sheep and goats (though they had relinquished cow sacrifice upon settling in India).

The reference to solar associations in the case of Findiriski is more complex. Those who might be tempted to take the reference literally would not have been highly regarded by Kaivan's circle. The Persian word for sun is *shams,* and probably the strongest dervish association here was the poetic tradition that incorporated metaphorical extensions of the historical episode of Shams-i Tabrizi, the teacher of Jalaluddin Rumi of Qonya. The "Sun of Tabriz" was a *qalandar,* that is, fitting the very broad category of a wandering dervish without affiliation to any dervish order. Yet more pertinent than *qalandari* associations here was the planetary lore of the Kaivanis, set against a broad frame of associations reminiscent of the ancient Sabeans in the encyclopaedic digest of the *Dabistan*. It is apparent that men of the intellectual finesse of Findiriski, Amili, Kaivan, and Farzaneh Behram ibn Farshad were quite capable of elaborating ancient star lore into a symbolic and initiatory shorthand forming an appendage to their widespread activities.

Nasr has had good cause to remark upon the enigmatic connections of Mir Findiriski with (Mulla) Sadruddin Shirazi (d.1640), who has been regarded by many as the leading philosopher of Safavid Iran. Some think that Sadra may have learnt much from his close contemporary Findiriski, but their acquaintance is not recorded. Findiriski's surviving treatises are faithful to the Peripatetic tradition, and hence appear to contrast strongly with Sadra's distinctive mixture of ishraqi, irfani (gnostic), peripatetic, and theological ingredients. Yet Findiriski's later fame as a sufi (and the extension as a Kaivani-ishraqi) means that he could have transmitted the more formal Peripatetic teaching while maintaining a sufi lifestyle.[8]

Findiriski was definitely a close personal acquaintance of both Amili and Mir Damad (d.1631), the latter being an ishraqi polymath and the teacher of Sadruddin Shirazi.

Though Findiriski gained court honours at Isfahan, he liked to wear coarse clothing and to mingle with the common people. Most biographical reports describe how the monarch Shah Abbas I (rgd. 1587–1629) tried on one occasion to admonish him for this fraternising with the commoner. The inference is valid enough that Findiriski did not esteem either formal learning or courtly behaviour; Nasr comments that Findiriski's manner resembled that of the Hindu yogis with whom he had extensive contact. His polymathy is demonstrated in his surviving works, which include a history of the Safavids, the *Usul al-Fusul* on the atypical subject of Hindu wisdom, a treatise on motion, and the *Risala-i-Sana'iyyah* (Treatise on Arts and Sciences). In the lastmentioned work, he takes to task those who overemphasize the differences in the expressions of wisdom of various sages, and who deny the underlying truth discernible in this apparent diversity. Findiriski instead maintained that all the "Greek" philosophers prior to Aristotle were describing the same reality in different languages; furthermore, those who are properly taught in the subtleties of Iranian *hiqmat* (wisdom philosophy), Hindu wisdom, and the *Theology of Aristotle* (i.e., the *Enneads* of Plotinus), will perceive all the different expressions of wisdom to have the same essential and perennial meaning.[9]

In the same treatise on the arts and sciences, Findiriski was particularly rigorous in his analysis of professional savants working in specialist departments of knowledge, e.g., physicians, engineers, and astronomers. With regard to such departments, he assigns a correct use and a misuse of each of these sciences. A separate category is reserved for those possessing only a theoretical knowledge of arts and sciences like music, medicine, or law, while he does not hesitate to criticize those who make a false claim even to theoretical knowledge. Such classifications seem every bit as relevant today (if not more so) than they were at the turn of the seventeenth century. The mere theoretician may commit less errors than those hard-nosed experimentalists who produce tangible monstrosities, while false claims to a theoretical knowledge of, e.g. music, has led to cacaphonies of progressive inertia.

The inference that Findiriski's conduct resembled that of Hindu yogis may be made more correct if it is added that it was Hindu sages and Zoroastrian ishraqis that he was emulating. It is certainly understandable that he should have deemed Mughal India a less hampered field of scope than the increasing Safavid persecution vogue that hallmarked the reign of Shah Abbas I, who savagely repressed "popular" Sufism. While Sadruddin Shirazi, alias Mulla Sadra, managed to steer a course clear of the court at Shiraz, even he had to be careful what he said; Findiriski evidently deemed long absences preferable from his Peripatetic role, though he was in Isfahan at the time of his decease.

Proof of other Muslim connections acquired by Azar Kaivan is afforded in the episode related by one Sayed Hasan Shirazi to the author of the *Dabistan*. (No clue is given as to the place of occurrence, but it is most likely to have been in India). Two members of a sufi sect or group went to meet Azar Kaivan, but did not treat him with due respect (they may have been jealous of his influence, or contemptuous of his Irani background). But afterwards the teacher of these two visitors had a dream in which the Prophet Muhammad affirmed that Kaivan was perfect in divine knowledge. This sufi preceptor then went himself to meet Kaivan, and was accompanied by Sayed Hasan Shirazi. Kaivan saluted his visitors in Persian and then began to converse in Arabic to the surprise of these Muslims. The *pir* described his dream, and Kaivan responded by telling him to keep that experience a secret.

Very little is known of Kaivan's early days in Iran, and it

is not even certain as to which country it was in that he went to a centre of learning and was able to answer every question put to him. As a result of this successful interrogation, the designation of "Master of the Sciences" (*Zhu'l-Ulum*) was conferred upon him. If this occurred in Iran, then he had evidently been successful by that time in the course of learning he had set himself in respect of the Iranian, Greek, and Indian heritages of wisdom. (Alternatively, even if the centre in question was one of the celebrated audience halls of Akbar at Fatehpur Sikri, we would not know owing to the absence of contextual data).

Kaivan's early course of learning did not merely consist of a formal acquaintance with texts. It is apparent that his disposition was highly contemplative. Modi aptly pointed out that the English translators of the *Dabistan* had wrongly rendered a meditative term as an actual place-name. For twenty-eight years Kaivan lived in "the abode in Khum" according to Shea and Troyer's version. The phrase should read "sat in *khum*," the last word of which literally means an earthen pot, but which signifies a posture of those practising *riyazat* (austerities) in sufi terms. Mobad Fardunji Marzban had more appropriately rendered *khum* as a "dark narrow place" in his Gujerati translation of the *Dabistan*, but even this is a questionable rendition.[10]

The report says that Kaivan would not allow his pupils to kill or injure animals, and that he himself would not eat meat. Yet he advised that each should adhere to their own religion. These details are compatible in the case of Muslims owing to the Akbarian policy, though it is not impossible that Kaivan himself was already accustomed to ascetic sustenance even before he arrived in India. Nor was vegetarianism completely unknown amongst Muslims prior to the reign of Akbar; the example of the freethinking poet Abu Ala al-Maari of much earlier times is one that springs immediately to mind. The question of to what extent Kaivan deliberately accommodated himself to the Akbarian policy is not easy to verify, but it is worth noting that the less elite Parsis had already tended to integrate to a substantial extent with the Hindu community. In 1580 Father A. Monserrate visited Navsari where Parsis were concentrated, but he could not distinguish them from Hindus, as his report confuses the two communities.

Exactly how Kaivan would have viewed Akbar is also an interesting subject, though speculative. He would doubtless have taken a dim view of Akbar's expansionist military policy throughout his reign, though the monarch seems to have been genuinely affected *c.*1575 by some experience which historians have felt obliged to describe as "mystical"; the monarch spent much time in prayer and meditation at this time in a manner that was markedly atypical for powerful emperors who could amuse themselves in practically any way they wanted. Yet Akbar's undoubted sympathy for mystical trends did not blind him to the shortcomings of some groups and cliques who opted for the limelight. It is reported by the contemporary chronicler Badauni that the monarch had a large number of *shaikhs* and *faqirs* despatched to remote Qandahar in Afghanistan, in exchange for horses, while members of a sect known as Ilahis were sent to the same region on the same basis of exchange.[11] These were conceivably cases of sending back rejects to the place of origin; the former contingent were doubtless "sufis" of the more motley variety who perpetuate attitudes and practices of a questionable educational value.

The *Dabistan* relates that a visitor to Kaivan expressed his intention of becoming a dervish. Kaivan briefly expressed his approval. Some days later the same visitor returned and said that he was now engaged in acquiring the various accoutrements necessary for the dervish life, items such as the patched robe, the dervish cap, the wallet. Kaivan replied: "The profession of a dervish consists in resigning everything and abandoning all manner of preparations, and not in accumulation of any kind."[12]

The externals of dervish lifestyles have too frequently taken precedent over essential qualities and objectives. Kaivan probably encountered too many persons preoccupied with preparatory rites to wish to see other than those who were serious thinkers or seekers.

Akbar was certainly not the only critic not to be fooled by the hypocrites. Owing to a lack of funds, a certain merchant assumed the garb of a sufi shaikh. Many people, mistaking the appearance for a reality, afterwards devoutly regarded him as a holy man. This shaikh came to Kaivan and said in justification that miscreants had often plundered him on the road, but that such misfortune had worked for his betterment, since by adopting the life of a dervish he could attain salvation. Kaivan soberly replied: "Be not grieved, as you are now plundering mankind by way of retaliation."[13]

It becomes more understandable why Kaivan maintained such an aura of seclusion, and enjoined secrecy upon his pupils. In a gullible climate, it is very easy to gain hordes of admirers who lack elementary capacities of perception; it is also very easy for copyists to pilfer elements of someone else's teaching and deform it in the process.

It is reported that the Kaivanis kept their teachings secret even from their own relatives. Their policy to strangers was highly distinctive for more than one reason. When anyone was introduced to their assemblies, they would praise his beliefs, approve whatever he said, and indeed heap upon him prodigious attention and respect. The *Dabistan* cautiously explains this phenomenon as the result of the Kaivani practice of not persuading any person to abandon his religious background, and that the group considered it unnecessary to cause any disturbance of mind to newcomers. Yet there may well have been deeper reasons. Upon close reflection, this was an effective method of concealment; it was also a potentially effective testing procedure for any demonstration of egotism that the newcomer was likely to express. Most people who are allowed to hold forth on their favourite hobby-horse will do so for rather a long time.

It is apparent that Kaivan was also capable of expressing reproof, however mildly or ingeniously, but then Kaivan was the leader of the group and such prerogative would not have been typical of his pupils.

An extremely atypical statement is found in the *Dabistan* which is refreshingly rare for a religio-mystical classic of philosophical dimensions: the Kaivanis refused to style the generality of mankind as wicked, and nor did they hold the worldly-minded in abhorrence, since the sentiment of abhorrence can only come from the envious.[14] The context is one related to the problem of those who cannot tell who is worldly-minded and who is not.

Though Kaivan doubtless held Akbar in respect, he is most unlikely to have considered Shah Abbas "the Great" of Iran as a model of excellence. The Safavid monarch's ruthless suppression of popular Sufism, for instance, was part of a campaign to secure monarchical supremacy that was in sharp contrast to the methods of Akbar. Whatever failings "popular" Sufism had, it had many good points that were singularly lacking in much court life. Flamboyant dervishes apart, many of the adherents of popular Sufism were artisans who lacked opportunities for further education and whose religious feelings were often blocked by the *ulama*; these artisans were often illiterate and contributed stunning workmanship for a mere pittance. Kaivan would have winced at some of the reports of oppression that percolated from Iran, and must have felt grateful that he was not within range of autocratic vindictiveness. He conceivably felt that the only positive contributions of Shah Abbas I were the improved national road system and the new city planning of Isfahan – which included the magnificent mosque known as the Masjid-i Shah, built during 1611–16 not by the monarch but by craftsmen who worked according to the plan created by Bahauddin Amili, the gnostic architect who was no stranger to Kaivani assemblies.

Azar Kaivan evidently had affinities with both the advanced Sufism of the Sunni world and the philosophical subtleties of the Shia world. Modi focussed upon the *Dabistan* report that someone (probably an exclusivist Sunni) expressed surprise to Kaivan that the Shi'is undercut the status of the early Caliphs Abu Bakr, Umar, and Uthman. A little ambiguously perhaps, Kaivan adroitly replied that the generality of people are influenced against the cause of truth by factors of "time and place." Less ambiguously, he added that these three early Caliphs had destroyed the ancient religion of the Iranians (i.e., Zoroastrianism), and therefore the Iranians, who had all adopted the Shia faith, had often been harbouring revolt against juristically standardized Islam. Modi interpreted this in the sense of Shia

Islam having retained elements of ancient Zoroastrianism.[15]

Modi observes that Kaivan taught transmigration (though in exactly what form is not on record), and deduced that the views of the Kaivan school were "somewhat sufistic with a mixture of Yoga." Was there, he asks, anything like Sufism among the ancient Mazdayasnian Persians? According to the *Dabistan*, there was. But Modi could not see how the ascetic strain was part of ancient Zoroastrianism, though he did concede that there was no categorical proof that transmigration was not a belief of some pre-Islamic Zoroastrians.[16]

What Modi, Erskine, and others classified as Sufism is actually a more complex phenomenon owing to its ishraqi components. Further, the increasing research on pre-Islamic Iranian religion does make it evident that an ascetic strain was a tangible ingredient of unorthodox, non-priestly Zoroastrianism.[17] Further, though it is often generalized that transmigration was never a concept promoted by Muslims, this is incorrect, since a minority of philosophers and sufis of Islamic background had been known to champion this concept in the earlier centuries of Islam.

Modi pertinently remarked that Patna may have become in Kaivan's day a renewed centre of old Indian philosophy and mysticism, and was here indicating not merely the Hindu heritage but also the Buddhist. Some of the earliest remains of Indian Buddhism are to be found in the Rajagriha Hills of the Patna district. At Panj Pahari, only about half a mile south of Patna, there stood some ancient ruins, the remnants of old Buddhist stupas or Jain cupolas. Some of the ruins were said to have antedated the reign of Chandragupta, who inaugurated the famous Maurya dynasty nearly two thousand years before Kaivan's time, a dynasty which patronized early Buddhism. The old palace of Chandragupta's capital Pataliputra stood at Kumrahar, near Patna.[18] Some will find it difficult to see how ancient Buddhist strains were necessarily involved in the Kaivani sequel at this site, but even if the suggestion is deemed a mere coincidental juxtaposition of associations, then it may still be appropriate in the sense of a recurrence. One of the missing books cited in the *Dabistan* refers to "Abadiyeh dervishes," which indicates a "Mahabadian" group probably synonymous with the Kaivani school. We have no details on the accommodation of the Kaivanis at Patna, nor of their aggregate lifestyle, but some of them at least may not have been so far removed from the disposition and curriculum of some of the early Buddhist monasteries, or proto-monasteries, in Mauryan and pre-Mauryan Bihar.

It was about 1580 that Akbar's policy resulted in a politico-religious crisis in the form of a revolt organized by orthodox Muslim reactionaries. The revolt was effectively overcome in 1581, and the monarch remained unchallenged for the last twenty-four years of his life. During that period he developed what a British historian has described as "an eclectic cult much influenced by Zoroastrianism and centred on himself." The main philosopher at the king's elbow was the Muslim Abu'l Fazl, who was an inspiration for a small circle of thinkers which included some Hindus. Some disagree with Spear that the details of this group are "not now of import," but it is true enough that Akbar's successor Jehangir retained some details which tended to glorify the monarch while discarding most of the attendant philosophy.[19]

Schimmel comments that the *din-i-ilahi* (Spear's "eclectic cult") can be called an order rather than a religion, though its usual translation is "divine faith." Central to the *din-i-ilahi* was the veneration of light, which may have had Zoroastrian roots, though one can find in it traces of the ishraqi tradition. Abu'l Fazl was responsible for reviving the Iranian concept of the *farr-i-izadi*, the *khvarenah* or glory (a very complex concept), and acknowledged this splendour as an attribute of Akbar. But it is important to understand that Akbar himself denied any claims to divinity. He arguably lived up to much of the dignity and clemency associated with the concept. He abolished the poll-tax (*jizya*) which Islamic legists exacted from the Hindus. He granted the city of Amritsar to Guru Ramdas, third guru of the Sikhs. He married Rajput princesses, but did not interfere with their Hindu religious customs, developments which made orthodox mullas complain of his adherence to infidel rituals in his palace. In 1587 the study of "useful sciences" began to be encouraged, outmanoeuvering the prevalent dominance of the customary curriculum of the Islamic ruling elite. Abu'l Fazl reports that Akbar was convinced that the fanatical hatred between Muslims and Hindus was a result of their mutual ignorance, which he wished to dispel by making the Hindu texts available to Muslims. He selected the Sanskrit epic *Mahabharata* as the most comprehensive (it is a vast work), and gave orders for it to be translated by scholars of both communities. In this way he wished to show the Hindus that some of their superstitions had no basis in their own ancient classics, and also to convince Muslims of their error in assigning the age of the world to a mere 7,000 years.[20]

Corbin has interpreted the Avestan term *khvarenah* (becoming in Persian *khurrah, farrah*) as "light of glory," representing an energy basic to the Mazdean view of the world that recurred in ishraqi teachings. This light, also known as *farr-i Yazdan,* is fundamentally an attribute in Zoroastrian lore of the symbolic entities known as amesha-spentas (and *izads*), but also acquired royal connotations in ancient Iran. Though a passage in the *Bundahisn*, the Zoroastrian Book of Creation, identifies *khvarenah* with the soul, it had achieved an iconographic extension in the luminous haloes awarded to priests and kings of the Zoroastrian tradition. This iconographic fashion was subsequently reaccentuated in the art of Mahayana Buddhism which depicted buddhas and bodhisattvas with an equivalent aureole.[21] It has sometimes been mistakenly identified solely with the relevant figures of Christian art, which is clearly derivative. Corbin also pointed out that the *khvarenah* forms the vermilion-gold background of many Manichaean paintings of Central Asian Turfan, and also of miniatures in some Iranian Islamic manuscripts of Safavid Shiraz, which he referred to as survivals of the mural paintings of the Sassanians.[22]

It is apparent that monarchical aspirations to deification achieved celebrity in ancient Iran, which must have served to heavily obscure earlier versions and aspects of the intrinsic Zarathushtran teachings. It has been pointed out that *khvarenah* is a concept not unknown in the Gathas, and is probably related to a psycho-mystical experience (or concepts) of inner light.[23]

With regard to the Mughal sequel to the ancient halo, it is arguable that the real genius behind effective developments at the court was Abu'l Fazl (or Abu'l Fazl and his closest confreres). Since it was not possible for them to achieve a dominant public focus themselves, they utilized the vehicle afforded by Akbar, whose borrowed halo was subsequently misused by later debauchees and ogres.

In this respect it is relevant that *khvarenah* also traditionally emerges as a quality that may adhere to kings and prophets, but departs from them if they are false to the principle of truth (*asha*).[24]

Even if Modi was correct in attributing the date of Azar Kaivan's arrival in India as late as *c.*1581 or closely following, then there is a possibility that his Yazdanian projection found its way into the more philosophical channels of Akbar's court, over and above the more ritualistic adjuncts of priests and theologians. Kaivan is likely to have deemed the kingly halo as much of an eccentricity as modern historians have done. Abu'l Fazl himself was no stranger to ishraqi views owing to his parental background, and conceivably expressed interest in the Patna contingent if he had not already done so at an earlier date.

The *Dabistan* only dwells very briefly on the ishraqi theme of "Oriental" and " Occidental" which has been a source of much speculation and argument amongst scholars. The Greek philosophers are divided into the "Oriental" and "Occidental" categories, with Plato and Aristotle as the respective foci; the "Oriental" philosophy is stated to be subsumed under the Azar-Hushangian sect, the leader of whom was Azar Kaivan.[25] Contrary to those generalizations which tend to align all "Islamic philosophy" with Plotinus owing to Porphyry's summary of the *Enneads* surviving in Arabic under the name of Aristotle, the ishraqi philosophers were well aware of Aristotelian methodology and incorporated it in their own methodology in an original manner that nevertheless allowed for the scientific extensions of logic. If some might choose to object that Plato was really Plotinus in the abovementioned characterization, it would not detract in the least from the essential implications.

Nasr has aptly remarked that European scholars have often overlooked, in relation to the vocalization of the Arabic word *mashriqiyah* ("oriental"), the wisdom of the Arabic language itself in affording the same root (*shrq*) to the words denoting "illumination" or "light" and "oriental", conforming to the obvious solar symbolism.[26] Though the subject has become controversial in relation to the terminology of the Peripatetic Ibn Sina, it is very rarely mentioned that in becoming a "sun-worshipper," Mir Findiriski and others were merely becoming true orientals in the spirit of illumination typifying the "realm of light" in the ishraqi tradition possessing pronounced Neoplatonic overtones.

The word ishraqi does of course come from the same root (*shrq*), or *sharq* as it was rendered by Modi, who translated *mashriq* in terms of "the rising of the sun in the East."[27]

It is evident that some of Kaivan's Zoroastrian disciples accompanied him to India from Iran. Others amongst them came to Patna from Iran, while one of them came to him from Surat and at least two were natives of Patna. Two of the early core of the group met him in Shiraz, while two others are reported to have first met him at Istakhar (near Persepolis), not far from Shiraz in the region of Fars. While the Shiraz locale is therefore the most likely place of origin for Kaivan, it is not definitively so.

The report of Kaivan's disciples in the *Dabistan* contains much hyperbole and symbolism. The hagiographical elements do not obscure the fundamental qualities depicted, and in many respects display a sophistication not always found in some of the contemporary sufi *tazkiras*. If there is any truth in Modi's dubious inference that the author was Farzaneh Behram ibn Farhad, then it may be that literary glosses and/or oral embellishments were later added. Such reworking is not untypical of such traditions. For instance, the extant *Zardusht-Afshar* comes from the pen (or dictation) of Mobad Sarosh, one of Kaivan's disciples. Yet it appears from the *Dabistan* that this Persian work is actually a commentary on an original written by Kaivan himself. In much the same way, Khuda Jui reworked Kaivan's *Mukashafat* ("Unveilings"), and it may even be that the *Desatir* represents a similarly recycled treatise from the Kaivan circle.

A prime example of embellishment is afforded by the case of Mobad Fardunji Marzban, who translated the *Dabistan* into Gujerati (published in Bombay in 1815). He was later reported to have demonstrated the lifestyle of a Kaivani-type sadhu,[28] but this apparent fidelity to precedent is no guarantee that Marzban was accurate in referring to Kaivan as a Dastur (high priest). It was Marzban who began this trend, which has no basis in the original Persian version of the *Dabistan*. Marzban's own priestly background was apparently the cause of the attribution.

There is also no proof that Kaivan was a *mobad* (priest of a fire temple). Revealing in this context is that, of the thirteen close Zoroastrian disciples of Kaivan described in the *Dabistan,* only six of them bear the sacerdotal title of *mobad.* The remaining seven were laymen. Modi points out that the designation of *farzaneh* was applied to five of these laymen; the epithet means "wise" or "learned," and seems to show that although these men were not priests, they had nevertheless acquired a redoubtable degree of learning and wisdom.[29]

Of the remaining two of the thirteen disciples, one was evidently a merchant. The movement as a whole acquired several merchants as members. Parsi traders were extremely industrious, and regularly moved between Gujerat, North India, and even Kashmir. It may well be that the mercantile members supplied funds for those who lived in comparative seclusion.

Modi attempted to pinpoint differences in aptitude amongst the Kaivanis. Interesting is his conclusion that some of them do not appear to have abstained from meat. These were the mercantile element, characterized by Modi as fringe followers. One does not feel that this is entirely correct, and the inference that some of the non-mercantile were doctrinaire while others resorted to ascetic practices without study can also be called into question. It seems more valid to concur with Modi that there were both learned and less learned Zoroastrian sufis represented, and that the Kaivani treatises incorporated (unorthodox) theological and dialectical ingredients. It is also relevant to add that after the death of Kaivan, there appears to have been an increasing diversity of affiliates, and that a number of groups were then in existence who can all be broadly termed Kaivani for purposes of ready reference. Further, some of the non-Zoroastrians who are described in the *Dabistan* in relation to Kaivan's circle of disciples were conceivably personal associates of Kaivan, e.g., Mir Findiriski. This is more definite for Bahauddin Amili, but Modi failed to integrate this detail.[30]

I propose to summarize here those individuals in the Kaivani groups of whom comparatively hard factual data has survived. The list is not exhaustive therefore.

In standardized sufi annals, one often finds a string of successors charted from the putative originator. This does not apply to the report of the Kaivanis, and later attributions are unsubstantiated.[31] This does not of course mean that there was no effective successor, but doubtless any such credentials were not advertised at the time.

Farzaneh Behram ibn Farhad (the elder Behram) came from Shiraz, and journeyed to Patna where he joined Kaivan's circle. This Zoroastrian was evidently an erudite man, fluent in Persian, Pahlavi, and Arabic, and conversant with various sciences and philosophies. He had been on personal terms with Jamaluddin Mahmud, who was a disciple of the Muslim ishraqi philosopher Jalaluddin Dawwani (d.1501/2). Behram ibn Farhad was evidently well informed in ishraqi matters. Though he practised austerities, he wore the garb of a small-time merchant rather than be pestered by the vulgar, who associated ishraqis with possession of the philosopher's stone and the knowledge of making gold. This literal version of alchemy had popularly adhered to Shaikh Sohravardi Maqtul after his death. Behram ibn Farhad was doubtless fluent in alchemical lore, but not as one of those "practising" alchemists who attempted to make gold, since this was considered a bovine pursuit by those of more developed intelligence. The Hermetic art was very much more cerebral in the ishraqi tradition than in other variants of the Graeco-Arabic heritage which achieved vogue from India to the British Isles. Yet despite the recourse of apparel, some onlookers thought that Farzaneh Behram was devoting himself in secret to literal alchemy. Externalism is sometimes a very deep-rooted affliction.

Before his death at Lahore in 1624, the elder Behram had written in Persian the *Sharistan-i-Danesh va Gulistan-i-Binash* ("The City of Knowledge and the Garden of Sight"), which is cited in the *Dabistan,* and which Modi identified with the extant *Sharistan-i-Chahar Chaman* ("The City of Four Gardens"). The author clearly knew Arabic, and notably quotes from the *Quran.* The work is divided into four *chamans* or "gardens," i.e., sections. It includes amongst its diverse contents a sequence of ancient prophets, and a section on cosmography which incorporates astronomical data.[32]

Another Zoroastrian disciple of Kaivan, Farzaneh Behram ibn Farshad (the younger Behram), was confused by Shea and Troyer with his close namesake Ibn Farhad. His linguistic skills were also extensive, since he knew Arabic, Persian, Hindi, and even Portuguese. The author of the *Dabistan* met him at Lahore prior to his death in that city in 1638. The *Dabistan* cites the younger Behram's treatise *Arzang-i-Mani* ("Gallery of Mani") unfortunately not extant, but whose title alludes to a well known Iranian legend concerning the gnostic leader Mani. But Behram ibn Farshad is more well known for acting as a translator of the writings of Shaikh Sohravardi Maqtul. These ishraqi classics he rendered from Arabic into Persian, though still with a strongly Arabicized flavour. Nasr has appropriately observed that Behram ibn Farshad's translation of Maqtul's *Hiqmat al-Ishraq* ("Wisdom of Illumination") belongs to an interesting but little studied aspect of the Kaivani movement that contributed to a major role of Sohravardi's concepts in the intellectual life of India up to the time of Muhammad Iqbal, and which resulted in some ishraqi writings coming to be known by Hindu scholars and sages.[33]

The *Hiqmat al-Ishraq* is the most famous work of Maqtul (still unavailable in an English translation), intricate in its style, and referring amongst other matters to the linkage of

Zoroastrian and Greek philosophical transmissions via the vehicle of what might be termed "high Sufism." The Greek component is associationally linked with the heritage of ancient Egypt.

One of the disciples who accompanied Kaivan to Patna from Iran was Farzaneh Kharrad (d.1620). This Zoroastrian had met Kaivan in a market of Shiraz. It was not a mercantile encounter however, since Kharrad had been practising *riyazat* (austerities) for several years, and hence already had some preparation for the counteracting of the automatic influences of "time and place."

Khuda Jui was a native of Herat (now in Afghanistan), but moved from that city in order to meet Kaivan at Istakhar in the Fars province of Iran.[34] He also knew both Arabic and Persian. He was apparently one of those who emigrated with Kaivan to India, all details of his training having escaped report. By the end of his life he was in Kashmir, where he arrived in 1631, and where the author of the *Dabistan* encountered him just prior to his death that same year. Closely associated with Khuda Jui was Mobad Khushi; these two men journeyed together to Istakhar to seek out Kaivan prior to emigrating to India. Previously, Khushi had searched from the time of his youth for a spiritual guide of the kind depicted in sufi lore. He was wide-ranging in his efforts, and travelled through Iran, Turkey, Central Asia, and India with this objective. He sought out not only Zoroastrians, but also Muslims, Jews, Christians, and Hindus. He met with much piety, but all of the venerated persons whom he encountered requested him to become converted to their own religion. The Zoroastrians were also insular in this respect. This continual and practically universal exclusivism offended him, and he felt that he should keep searching rather than to give in to a local set of assertions. In Azar Kaivan he did not find this exclusivism – the Zoroastrian disciples of this philosopher did not regard themselves as adherents of the "Zoroastrian faith," but rather as the inheritors of a lengthy convergence of philosophical and religio-mystical traditions. Furthermore, they did not view the Zoroastrian tradition in the orthodox manner even when they chose to focus upon it in their treatises.

In brief, this grouping exemplified in no uncertain manner the perspective which is sometimes identified nowadays with the "perennial philosophy," or in a more scholastic idiom, *philosophia perennis* or *theosophia perennis*. Twentieth century views on this subject tend to be prone to various constrictions caused by such factors as a tendency to obscurantism, a distinct lack of critical acumen with respect to historical features, a neglect of discrimination that is prejudicial to ancient priorities extant in texts, and a confusion in certain avenues concerning the interlocking of different traditions.[35]

According to the *Dabistan,* Mobad Parastar died suddenly in Kashmir in 1640 while in the ascetic position of standing on his head. This might well be taken as a warning in the adoption of yogic *asanas* or postures, which enthusiasts are perenially prone to overdo and overexhibit. The author of the *Dabistan* relates that he had actually met Parastar in Kashmir, and therefore the report of the latter's death may not be readily regarded as fiction. Parastar was a disciple of Kaivan, though born in Patna unlike many of his Zoroastrian comrades. His Zoroastrian father had been a merchant of Isfahan background and had chosen to settle in Patna, though not it seems for Kaivani purposes. By contrast, the son was "upside down in orientation to the world" to use a sufi phrase indicative of the reversal in priorities from mundane incentives.

The brother of Parastar was "Mobad" Peshkar, likewise born in Patna, and likewise a pupil of Kaivan. The *Dabistan* similarly stresses his ascetic practices, e.g. breath control, and reports that he became an expert in Hindi songs and verse. It is evident that he was well acquainted with Hindu and yogic lore, and it may well be that he also had an interest in Buddhism. He accompanied his brother to Kashmir, intending to go from there to North China. Modi inferred that Peshkar must have succeeded in this intention. Since there is no indication that Peskhar was a merchant, but rather an ascetic, it is not impossible that he investigated Mahayana Buddhism in Ming China – not because of any personal need to do so, but owing to the extensions of activity amongst increasing Kaivani groups.

In China at that time was an increasing eclecticism of the different traditions of Buddhism, and an attendant trend towards laymen gaining dominance as teachers in contrast to ordained monks. These features parallel the apparent lay element in the Kaivani circle. Further, the chief Chinese exponent of these developments was a close contemporary of Kaivan. I am referring to Chu-hung (1535–1615), a Buddhist monk who attempted to counteract the degeneration of the *sangha* (monastic order); he was conversant with the diverse teachings of the Hua-yen, Ch'an, and Pure Land traditions, though he stressed that the popularity of Ch'an (Japanese: Zen) Buddhism had caused the deterioration of monastic discipline. Chu-hung was mainly active in South China, but his influence was widely felt throughout China by the seventeenth century. He became involved in a dispute with the Jesuits who had recently arrived in China, and who selected Buddhism as their main rival amongst the Chinese.[36] Some of the Kaivanis were particularly adroit at avoiding arguments between religious factions, but in China Peshkar would have sympathized with the Chinese side of the dispute owing to the *ahimsa* contentions.

It was Peshkar's brother Parastar who wrote the *Tapreh-i-Mobadi,* a work not extant, but whose title Modi translated as "The Path of making *tap* for mobads."[37] *Tap* is here considered synonymous with *riyazat* (austerities), the former word being the root for the Sanskrit word *tapas,* meaning approximately "heating," in the sense of an ascetic discipline. But there is an ancient warning attendant upon the practice of intensive disciplines and exercises; Eliade has aptly observed that the superhuman power acquired by the ascetic *sadhaka* "can become terrible and in certain cases 'demonic'."[38] Further, the inexpert application of some exercises can cause unpleasant effects for the practitioner, resembling what might perhaps best be termed a psychic shock.

Both Parastar and Peshkar held in high esteem another disciple of Kaivan. This was Sarosh ibn Kaivan ibn Kamgar, reportedly another *mobad,* who was still alive in Kashmir in 1627, when he was aged sixty. He lived a celibate life, and had travelled extensively. He had learnt

"Arab culture" from the elder Behram, possibly a reference to Quranic text and the traditions of the Prophet Muhammad known as *hadith.* His linguistic achievements were typically broad in that he knew Arabic, Persian, and Hindi. He wrote at least three books,[39] though it is mainly miracles that are related of him in the *Dabistan.* For example, it is stated that he understood the language of animals and vegetables and minerals; more ecological sympathies in today's world would undoubtedly be beneficial for humans also. More perplexing to contemporary evaluation is the assertion that "Mobad" Sarosh had the power to revive the dead *and* to deprive the living of life. The power to kill is sometimes attributed to saints and others in sufi and Hindu literature, but it is a less well known interpretation that those *sadhakas*[40] who become dangerous (both to themselves and to others) can be effectively dealt with by their superiors, whether or not these latter are acknowledged to be such.

When Sarosh's pupil Yazdan Sitai heard from a servant of the Kaivani merchant Shidosh that he (the servant) had been hurt by the local inhabitants at a place in Kashmir, Sitai vengefully invoked rain to destroy the properties of the offenders by floods. (It seems that he had gained a yogic reputation for paranormal powers). But when Sarosh heard of this act of wrath, he was angry with his pupil for giving vent to this form of retaliation; he accordingly rebuked Sitai and altered the effects of the curse. Later, when the same hapless servant complained to Sarosh himself of having been ill-treated by the inmates of a caravanserai in a Central Asian city, Sarosh is reported to have merely caused apparitions of very large men to appear before the miscreants in order to frighten them and deter them from molesting others.

Hushiyar is one of those amongst Kaivan's Zoroastrian disciples who can be termed a Parsi, since he is reported to have come to Patna from Surat in Western India. He wrote at least one book, and is referred to as a *mobad.* He was amongst those whom the author of the *Dabistan* knew personally, and from childhood. It seems questionable as to whether some (or even any) of the men designated as *mobads* in Kaivan's circle bore any resemblance to practising priests as was then customary in Parsi usage of the term. In the view of the present author, it is more likely that the nomenclature of the Kaivani group transposed the orthodox term into one of initiatory significance. This does not mean that some of them did not have priestly ancestors (or even that some of them may have started their career as priests), but it does mean that the title of *mobad* (priest of a fire temple) when applied to them is misleading if construed literally. The author of the *Dabistan* evidently delighted in various forms of nuance, apparent in other Kaivani treatises also. (Even the title of the *Dabistan,* or rather *Dabistan-i-Mazahib,* has been the subject of different interpretations).[41]

The title of *mobad,* which derives from Old Persian *magupati,* was in use during the Sassanian era, but is not clear in the signification then given to it. The earlier Parthian variant of *magbad* may have designated the chief priests of fire temples, in continuation of Achaemenid usage.[42] Since it is apparent from Kaivani treatises that the "sacred fire" lore had extensions in the "self-burning" concept, it is not impossible that the style of *mobad* in Kaivani usage had overtones of a maturity in this concept. The ambivalence of the Kaivani use of the *mobad* title is also reflected in the extant name of the *Dabistan* author, since a well known manuscript declares "Mobad Shah" to have been his poetical name.[43]

Prior to his death in 1640 at Agra, Hushiyar the *mobad* was clearly on good terms with influential Hindu ascetics. It was he who took the *Dabistan* author (when the latter was an infant) in 1618–19 to Balk (Balik) Natha, a yogi who was evidently connected with the Kaivani core group. This incident could have occurred in the Patna region, before "Mobad Shah" moved with his relatives and their associates from Patna to the capital of Agra (Akbarabad), which seems to have taken precedence over Patna for at least a section of the Kaivanis. It seems to have been in the Agra locale that the *Dabistan* author was taken by his mentor Hushiyar to visit Chatur Vapah, a brahmin ascetic,[44] in the year 1623. This Hindu sage was well known in the area, and an important clue is afforded to one of the probable links in terminology achieved by the Zoroastrian and Muslim ishraqis in their interchanges with the Hindus. Chatur Vapah is stated by "Mobad Shah" to have taught him the "*mantra* of the sun." Exactly what this was is not specified, but it was no secret in those days that the *Gayatri mantra* was of an extremely old Vedic provenance; this verse from the *Rig-Veda* was dedicated to the solar deity Savitri and was regarded as the most sacred verse in Hindu scripture[45]:

Tat Savitur vareniam
Bhargo devasya dhimahi
Dhiyo yo nah pracodayat.

("Let us meditate on the supernal light of Savitri, and may this Light illumine our minds").

This "illumining light" was equatable, by extension, with certain of the *shrq* concepts of the ishraqiyun.

Chatur Vapah is said to have appointed one of his own pupils to look after the young "Mobad Shah" until he came of age. It is therefore not unreasonable to surmise that the boy resided at, or near, a Hindu *ashram* of Kaivani affiliation, until his subsequent move to Kashmir where he was in close association with other "mobads" by 1627. This detail apart, it is evident on the basis of the yogi Balk Natha that Hindu affiliates were already a distinctive feature of Kaivani activity by the time of Azar Kaivan's death. This means that it is not in order to consider Ram Bhat as necessarily the first Hindu Kaivani. Ram Bhat was a brahmin of Benares, and is reported in the *Dabistan* as a disciple of Farzaneh Behram ibn Farhad; it was he who caused many other Hindus to become pupils of this elder Behram.

This substantial Hindu influx is therefore dateable to the approximate period of 1618–24. Since Ram Bhat came from Benares, this is possibly of significance with regard to known developments in that centre of Hinduism. It was in Benares during this period that one of the major Hindu saints died. This was Tulsi Das, and the traditional date for his death is 1623. Much of his biography is traditionalized in the conventional manner of *bhakti* devotionalism, but certain details do emerge with reasonable clarity. Whaling infers that Tulsi Das was a reformer, though not of the radical category that hallmarks Kabir and Nanak. He does not show evidence of having inveighed against the caste structure like his predecessors, but he did outmanoeuvre the priestly form of composing in Sanskrit, long since a "dead" language for the caste and non-caste public at large. His famous *Ramacharitamanas* was a reworking of the Sanskrit epic *Ramayana*. It was written in Avadhi, an eastern Hindi dialect, and served to mediate the classical ideal of the *avatar* Rama to a very wide audience of non-Sanskrit speaking Hindus. Though traditions have it that saints like Sur Das and Mira Bai (a Rajput woman who is very difficult to date) recognized Tulsi's authority, the brahmins of Benares tended to regard it as an insult that he used the vernacular Hindi instead of the classical tongue.[46] It is difficult to say to what extent the brahmins of Benares maintained their resistance, but Ram Bhat was evidently one of those who decided that Hindi was not inferior, even if it carried pronounced Arabo-Persian overtones.

Several of the disciples of Azar Kaivan could speak Hindi, and it is deducible that they threw in their weight to the anti-ritual and *ahimsa* features of the *bhakti* movement.

Many Westerners seem incapable of understanding Hindu *bhakti* (devotion), but as Jordens observed, it was the influence of Tulsi Das that stretched into the twentieth century to cause Gandhi to cry out "He Ram!" when he was hit by the fatal bullets of the assassin.[47]

Shidosh ibn Anosh is one of those listed in the *Dabistan* as a close disciple of Kaivan. His lifestyle displayed marked differences to that of his comrades. He and his Zoroastrian brother Zarbadi were at first both destitute, and asked Kaivan for his advice. He told them to go, with a small capital, to the country of the rising sun, i.e. to the East, and afterwards return to the country of the setting sun, i.e. the West. The report shows signs of ishraqi metaphor, and it is possible therefore that Kaivan gave these two Zoroastrians (or one of them) a "double" instruction intended to apply to both their psychological and mundane careers. In ishraqi symbolism, the "East" represents the sector of illumined consciousness, while the "West" signifies the material world, which is shrouded in darkness and ignorance, but which can be aligned with the "world of light" in the individual process of conscious development.

Whatever the complexities of the instruction, it appears that Shidosh and his brother afterwards travelled to distant Far Eastern countries for trading purposes. It may be that Chinese Turkestan was the area of focus here, since the *Dabistan* refers to Kashgar as an intended objective for Shidosh. From the time he left Patna, his mind was flooded with spiritualizing thoughts, causing him to adopt the obscure practice of *Awad-Azad,* as the *Dabistan* refers to it in Persian. A Hindu synonym of *anahad* is also given; it is probable that this was a Kaivani method of discipline known by convenient abbreviations. During the sojourn of these brothers in distant territories, Azar Kaivan's death occurred at Patna. It was not Zarbadi, but Shidosh who subsequently gained esteem amongst the Kaivani groups. The author of the *Dabistan* personally encountered Shidosh in Kashmir, while the former was still in his youth, and reports that Shidosh had become a wealthy merchant, and dressed in worldly magnificence. Yet Shidosh was quite frank in stating that he owed his worldly wealth to his teacher Azar Kaivan, and hence he had to put this wealth to good use. He related to the young "Mobad Shah" that the "heavenly light" had been revealed to him; this is an ishraqi allusion, and refers to a state of mind achieved after a successful course of discipline under a competent teacher (in contrast to an unsuccessful course of discipline under an incompetent teacher, whatever the sensations attendant upon such an avenue). It is probable that some would have considered Shidosh to be too worldly for holy man status; yet he appears to have made no specific pretence of being holy. Modi commented that Shidosh appears to have been "a mystic recluse in the midst of the world,"[48] which is a simple way of saying that the West had become oriented to the East.

When Shidosh was afflicted with illness in Kashmir, he remained cheerful. He even consoled his friends, telling them that he was going to a better world. He would recite couplets from Shaikh Muhammad ibn Abdulla Nurbakhsh (d.1465), an Iranian dervish leader whose followers and purported followers had been active in Kashmir.[49] Shidosh died from his illness in 1629, on Kashmiri soil.

Another Kaivani with whom the *Dabistan* author personally conferred was Sayed Muhammad al-Isfahani (d. 1634). The latter is not specified as a pupil of Kaivan, but as a pupil of Farzaneh Behram ibn Farhad. This Muslim of good birth was treated with typically courteous respect upon his first visit to Farzaneh Behram, who gave him a seat of honour that was somewhat higher than those taken by others on that occasion. A naked *faqir* subsequently entered (this unnamed entity could have been either a *qalandar* or *sadhu*), and was awarded a comparatively inferior place in the room. The sayed felt that there was something wrong in this disparate arrangement. Farzaneh Behram then turned his face to the wall, which was decorated with paintings or carpets, and mused aloud: "Though a form may be accommodated with distinction, external forms are imperfect. Yet dervishes gain real rank when their souls gain control of their bodies. In this assembly such dervishes are dear to my heart."

Al-Isfahani later explained to "Mobad Shah" that this episode was the cause of his turning to the right path[50] (which involved a comparative lack of self-esteem).

A less socially elevated Muslim who became a pupil of one of the Behrams was Mahmud Beg Tamin, who was an illiterate Turk. Though men of his background were often recruited into military ranks as "men of the sword," Mahmud Beg adopted the *ahimsa* practices of the Kaivanis. The *Dabistan* reports of him that upon seeing a dog in pain, he purchased medicine for the creature by selling his prayer rug and rosary, and was successful in the cure. This was in sharp contrast to the more unintelligent Muslim indifference to dogs. Boyce has observed that early Islam knew nothing of the later Muslim hostility to the dog as an unclean animal, a hostility which seems to have been deliberately fostered in Iran owing to the high degree of respect for dogs that was displayed by Zoroastrians. Boyce feasibly infers that maltreatment of the dog was encouraged by zealots as a sign of true conversion, along with such gestures as spitting into a sacred fire of the gabrs (infidels).[51] There was nothing ecological in this aversion; this behavioural extreme was caused by religious rivalry, and is a good (or bad) example of zealot habits of mind determining inferior conduct.[52]

Lahore became the centre of the activities of Farzaneh Behram the younger. In this city of the Punjab, and well into the reign of Shah Jahan, the Kaivani-ishraqi influence appears to have moved axis from the Patna locale. It did meet with initial resistance from Mulla Sayed Muhammad al-Samarqandi, who doubtless thought that Farzaneh Behram was a mere fire-worshipping infidel, and therefore wrong in whatever he said. This *mulla* bestirred himself to visit Behram in Lahore, with the intention of ridiculing him, but when he came into the presence of his imagined foe, the *mulla* lost his sense of antagonism, and instead bowed low at Behram's feet. Unfortunately there are no details of what happened afterwards, and so we do not know whether the *mulla* chose to become a pupil or merely decided to keep his distance and not wrangle with someone more learned and dynamic than he was.

Another zealot of whom there is data concerning the sequel was a Portuguese Christian whose name is reported as Antun Bashuyah Vavraj. He is described as a "Frank" (*farangi*), the term reserved for Christians amongst Persian-speakers. This Antoine may have been affiliated to the Jesuits; he was evidently an orthodox Christian of evangelical inclinations and owned extensive property. But after meeting Behram ibn Farshad, he renounced his riches and took to the life of a vagrant *qalandar,* with the further refinement that he went naked in the manner of Hindu sadhus. His teacher Behram always referred to him as "Messiah," perhaps a reference to his former zealousness which he was now effectively altering. Antoine the *qalandar* did not push his views it seems, and was thorough in the application of his new-found ideals. He was once beaten up by some roughneck, and the *Dabistan* author was one of those who found him afterwards. Antoine is then reported to have remarked: "I feel distressed that my attacker's hands and fists must have suffered so much in hitting me."[53]

Gandhi would probably have applauded this seventeenth century precendent of *satyagraha*. It seems that in order to emulate Christ and Francis of Assisi during the seventeenth century, it was necessary to go to India and become a Kaivani *qalandar*. Even Galileo might have been impressed had he been able to see the episode with his own eyes.

It is not known whether Behram ibn Farshad's extensive linguistic expertise extended to Hebrew, but Christians were not the only "foreigners" to receive his benign attention. There were (at least) two Jews amongst his pupils, namely Musa and Harun. Neither of them were illiterate since they were rabbis, and hence not easily convinced of extraneous views. They evidently preferred to lead a non-dogmatic existence, at least on a part-time basis, since they opted for mercantile activity. It would be rash to infer from this detail that they were "fringe followers"; if the example of Shidosh ibn Anosh is anything to go by, then he was considered to be more advanced than some of the outright ascetics.

The author of the *Dabistan* appears to have moved between the Kaivani group (or groups) in Kashmir and the Lahore circle during the period extending from the late 1620's until the 1640's, by which time he was also active in Gujerat.[54] By that time the younger Behram had died, and there is no clue afforded to any specific role of leadership. However, this latter factor would doubtless not have been broadcast. Mobad Shah appears to have gone to Mashhad in 1643, which would tend to indicate his close connection with Shia Muslims. Troyer tentatively ascribed to him the conjoint role of a travelling merchant and philosopher. This is not impossible, but there is no proof of the former aspect of vocation any more than there is of a priestly one.

The *Dabistan* was not finished until the mid-1650's, and by that date the author had ample time to include reference to three individuals who cannot be definitively categorized as "Kaivanis," though they were evidently in close contact with Kaivani activity. The distinctions of labelling would have been deemed irrelevant by all of them.

Hakim Dastur is a name that is almost a contradiction in terms, particularly when its owner is described as a merchant. He travelled extensively, relates the *Dabistan,* in accordance with the custom of merchants. Dastur is the title for a Zoroastrian high priest, but this august sacerdotal category do not adopt the mercantile role. *Hakim* is an Arabic word that generally designates a Muslim sage, but more specifically at this era in the Iranian milieu, it became associated with the exponents of a complex fusion of ishraqi, peripatetic, and *irfani* (gnostic) philosophy, a fusion that is most well known in the works of Sadruddin Shirazi (d.1640).[55] Yet this latter category is generally conceived of as perpetuating the sedate lifestyle of the more scholarly and liberal Mullas, and not that of itinerant merchants. What then is the explanation for these apparent anomalies?

Though we cannot be definitively certain of Hakim Dastur's religious background, he is more likely to have been a Zoroastrian than a Muslim in view of the priestly tag. But the title of Dastur was probably a metaphorical recasting of prerogative in the philosophical field, even if his parentage was of the formal sacerdotal kind. That the subject was a philosopher is categorical enough in view of the *Dabistan* assertion that Hakim Dastur followed the rule of the *mashsha'iyun* (Peripatetics). Further, he had come to India from Shiraz, where he had been intimate with Mir Muhammad Baqir Damad (d.1631) and other learned men in that city. Hakim Dastur's actual birthplace was Balkh, in Central Asia, though his family originated in Isfahan. He did not arrive in Lahore until 1644–5.[56]

Brief though the details are, it seems a valid extrapolation that the *hakims* of that era were not all tied to desks or mosque pulpits; the itinerant variety are almost completely unknown, but conceivably hold the answer to the complexities of interaction between Safavid Iran and Mughal India at philosophical levels. The more sedentary activities at Isfahan and Shiraz were clearly complemented by the more mendicant and itinerant phases of such as Findiriski, Amili, and Hakim Dastur.

The last years of Mir Damad seem to have passed in close association with ishraqi events at Shiraz. The *Tarikh-i Alam Ara-yi Abbasi,* written in 1616, describes Mir Damad as skilled in most of the sciences, particularly philosophy, philology, mathematics, medicine, and law. Though he had been actively engaged in scholastic discussions and theological polemics, Bazmee Ansari comments that Damad rose morally above most of his contemporaries engaged in "petty jealousy and mutual disparagement."[57]

Mir Damad is an important figure in the philosophical events and interactions of the early Safavid era, despite the extremely difficult style of his writings which made him (intentionally) laborious to read by both his contemporaries and later researchers. Nasr states that Damad's closest friend at the Safavid court was Bahauddin Amili, though he is not known to have travelled widely like the latter. But Damad was the teacher of Sadruddin Shirazi, and more than anyone else, Damad was responsible for the revival of Peripatetic philosophy (in the Avicennian guise) and the ishraqi wisdom philosophy within the nascent form of state religion Shi'ism. He revived what he referred to in his complex terminology as the Yamani (Yemeni) wisdom. This *falsafih-i-Yamani* is synonymous with the ishraqi wisdom of illumination (*hiqmat al-ishraq*), with Yemen symbolizing the right or oriental (*mashriqi*) side of the metaphorical valley,[58] which it is necessary to cross over in the journey from darkness to light.

Returning to the pages of the *Dabistan*, it is there found reported that the author knew a philosopher named Hirbed, whom he visited in Lahore. Hirbed had also come from Shiraz, where he had learnt the sciences; he was well versed in the works of Sohravardi Maqtul, which "he made his own, both in spirit and word" to borrow an apt phrase from Shea and Troyer. Hirbed was not a Muslim but a Zoroastrian, and is described as a descendant of the family of Zardusht (Zarathushtra) in accord with the genealogical parlance of the *Dabistan*. There is no mention of any mercantile activity in his case; on the contrary, the *Dabistan* specifically refers to Hirbed as leading an austere life (though it is obvious that the two lifestyles do not necessarily conflict, e.g., the case of the Prophet Muhammad and his annual retreats to Mount Hira). Hirbed was another ishraqi with an extensive linguistic range; he not only composed verses in Persian, Arabic, and Hindi, but also held conversations with learned *farangis,* i.e., the Portuguese.

No date is given for his arrival in India, but it may have been while Farzaneh Behram the younger was still alive at Lahore, in which case they would appear to have had much in common.[59]

More well known in Indian annals than either Hirbed or Hakim Dastur is Sarmad, though still comparatively overshadowed by regal events, and not at all well known in the West. Sarmad was an Armenian Jew, the descendant of a family of rabbis, and appears to have mastered the Hebrew language and its rabbinical literature. But he was something of a freethinker, and he later studied the New Testament and other books on Christianity. The earlier part of his life was spent at Kashan, an Iranian centre of crafts and trade, and he adopted a mercantile livelihood at some unknown date, possibly as a result of a flourishing parental business. His freethinking tangent led him to Shiraz, where he became a pupil of Sadruddin Shirazi and Mir Findiriski. The influence of his environment caused him to become a Muslim, but his grounding in Jewish scholarly tradition remained deep. As Rizvi remarks, Muhammad Sa'id Sarmad had very strong affinities with *ishraq* and *wahdat al-wujud,* the latter pantheistic philosophy being associated with the name of Ibn al-Arabi (d.1240), the Spanish Arab of gnostic fame. The latter tradition is extremely complex and generally simplified in much modern literature; suffice it to say here that it was known in Iran as *irfan,* but it was also well known (and popularized) in Sunni countries.

Next to nothing is known of Sarmad's acquaintance with Findiriski and Shirazi. The biography of Sarmad is heavily dependent upon the *Dabistan,* which dwells with typical and oblique brevity upon details deemed digestible for its audience. Findiriski has been mentioned above, but of Sadruddin Shirazi, alias Mulla Sadra, there exists both more information and more confusion in interpretation. While it is now well known that the nineteenth century diplomat and scholar Comte Arthur de Gobineau mistakenly considered Sadra's major philosophical treatise to be a series of books on travel, other contractions and distortions require to be reappraised.

Mulla Sadra (1571/2–1640) denounced the scholastic

approach of the orthodox *ulama* to the study of religion, and particularly to philosophy. It was early in his career that he openly expressed his belief in a pantheistic perspective of the universe, and reaffirmed the unorthodox views of Sohravardi Maqtul as taught by his instructor Mir Damad. But Mir Damad, despite the respect awarded him by the monarch on account of his polymath learning, met with censorship from Shia clerics (if anybody is still wondering why his style of writing was so abstruse, then they should project themselves back into the era in question). Sadra himself was constrained to escape religious persecution by a flight to a small village near Qum, where he stayed in very quiet retreat for a substantial length of time that varies from seven to fifteen years depending upon the source consulted. By the time that he wrote his famous *Al-Hikma al-muta'aliya fi' asfar al-aqliya al-arba'a* (Gobineau's "travel" book), he soberly reflected in the introduction that solitary confinement had caused him to realize how he had rendered himself in the wrong by relying too greatly upon his intellectual powers. Yet this adroit concession to the orthodox was accompanied by the statement that intense contemplation had enabled him to comprehend intuitively what he had previously learned rationally.

(Sadra was subsequently reinstated to a position of eminence in Shiraz, where he did his best through the channels afforded him to promote and project a rich combination of ishraqi, gnostic, and Peripatetic philosophy that can sound disarmingly simple to anyone who does not read it closely or familiarize themselves with the relevant terminology).

Sadra has drawn the criticism of modernists by his unambiguous statement in his *Sa fasl* that true knowledge is accessible only to the initiated, meaning the chosen few who have to protect this knowledge and hence conceal it from the uninitiated.[60] Apart from the irony implicit here as to who the true knowledge was being guarded from, even such distant contemporaries as Kepler and Galileo must have occasionally felt that they were the true elect whose knowledge was effectively concealed from the religious and scholastic establishments alike, not to mention Sir Isaac Newton who clearly felt that there was an "initiatory" chain of knowledge devolving from Pythagoras and was accordingly extraordinarily secretive over his alchemical studies.[61] If such was the case with Newton, then surely due latitude can be extended to an even earlier Iranian savant?

It has been urged that the excommunication of philosophers like Mulla Sadra rarely affected the life and work of the stigmatized heretic, "except possibly in terms of forced social isolation." This may actually be true, but only because such individuals took the precautions that they did, e.g., involved and complex writings, and varying degrees of an attempted compatibility with Shia orthodoxy. However, if it be considered elitist that such philosophers escaped with their lives by using their above average wits, then what is the position of modern academics and other persons of eminence who do not express views or opinions in any way differing from the customary norm? What would be the modern equivalent of Mulla Sadra's categoric denial of the physical resurrection of the body, his emphatic refutation of the theological conceptions of a physical afterlife? How many modern academics would willingly or stoically face the prospects of "forced social isolation"? They are not all Wittgensteins.

It has been pointed out that despite his manifestation of piety, Mulla Sadra was frequently attacked by some of the exoteric *ulama,* who denounced him publicly more than once; it was only through the influence of his powerful family that it was possible for him to continue teaching at Shiraz during the last phase of his career.[62]

Bayat has observed that Mulla Sadra criticized the narrowmindedness, the ignorance, and the stifling cultural attitude of those *ulama* who maintained a literal traditionalism and who refused to interpret religion in any other way than the exoteric. In his own esoteric version, Sadra notably employed technical sufi language. Yet he never belonged to any dervish order. On the contrary, he also criticized the (nominal) sufis for their lack of interest in philosophical inquiry, and wrote a treatise which refuted various "sufi" practices and beliefs.

This latter detail is liable to distortion if not sufficiently clarified. Arjomand has described Mulla Sadra as the representative *par excellence* of *both* the gnostic/philosophical and the eremitic/ascetic sufi outlook of that era. In his *Kasr Asnam al-Jahiliyya* ("Breaking the Idols of Ignorance"), Sadra became the representative of "high Sufism" and aimed a critical volley at the "low Sufism" in general manifested by the dervishes and *qalandar* types (some of these being very aberrant). He rigorously denounced in this work the charlatanry, worldliness, orgiasticism, and the superstitious thaumaturgy of the popular version of the sufi phenomenon.[63]

This data is afforded a clearer relief by certain social and monarchical trends. For instance, either just before, or during, Sadra's retreat to a rural area, he might conceivably have heard of a grisly episode which is credibly reported in the *Tarikh-i Abbasi* of Falsafi: an Uzbek was eaten alive by the executioners at the order of Shah Abbas I in 1602. This reported cannibalism is rendered more indigestible to the sufi perspective owing to the fact that the cannibals were "sufis" of the warrior-like *qizilbash* contingent whom the monarch had been squeezing into his schemes of supremacy. This royal policy was what resulted later that century in the reports of Christian missionaries that sufis still wearing traditional headgear were regarded as riff-raff in Persia, serving as royal guards, employed as menials in royal buildings, and filling the role of executioners. This debacle of popular Sufism was closely linked with the fortunes of the Safavid order of dervishes, whose membership included the Turkmen *qizilbash* who were employed as a military faction by Shah Ismail, founder of the Safavid dynasty in the early sixteenth century, i.e., the leader of the order of dervishes became the monarch of Iran, repressing other dervish orders in the process. By the time of Shah Abbas I, the monarch had decided that the *qizilbash* sufis and others needed to be more docile to the monarchical spur. While many of them were brought to heel by filling convenient roles of subservience to the *murshid* (i.e. the monarch), he did not hesitate to massacre some of them in 1614, "the old sufis of Lahijan" being accused of collaboration with the Ottomans and of failure to be loyal to the will of the *murshid* (i.e. the monarch) before all other worldly interests. This massacred contingent were the oldest adherents of the Safavid order of dervishes,[64] and hence a thorn in the side of the *murshid,* possibly reminding him of the less regal origins of his position and authority.

There may well be more than one version of the elite, and possibly sufis like Mir Findiriski were necessary in order to counteract the influence of false and despotic sufis.[65]

Sarmad, the pupil of the *murshids* Mulla Sadra and Findiriski, was probably still a young man during his Shiraz phase. The first definite date in his life is that of 1632–3, when he landed at Tatta on the coastline of Sind in northwest India. By that time he was a wealthy man, having accumulated substantial riches owing to his participation in the prosperous trade then operative between Iran and India. Sarmad appears to have followed the general trend of migration to Indian soil of Iranian merchants, scholars, and philosophers, some of whom were undoubtedly seeking a less oppressive climate rather than lucrative opportunities. Though he appears to have arrived in India as a merchant (or more probably a merchant and *hakim*), he definitely did not remain a trader. The details are very scanty, and have been misconstrued. Sarmad renounced his riches and became a *qalandar* in the literal sense of the term, i.e., a dervish who disregards appearance and is heedless of local opinion. In this he seems to compare closely with the correct use of the idiom by Antoine Bashuyar the Christian Kaivani. Sarmad is said to have gone naked, a practice of some Hindu sadhus. This change approximately coincided with his encounter with a Hindu boy known as Abhai Chand, who belonged to a family of *vaishya* caste Hindus. This was apparently in Tatta, and the family were possibly mercantile. The *Dabistan* is vague in its indications that Sarmad took to the role of a *qalandar* owing to his frustration at loss of contact with Abhai Chand, whose parents concealed him from the stranger. It seems more likely that when Sarmad became a *qalandar,* he wanted to take on Abhai Chand as a pupil, recognizing the boy's talent and genius. The parents eventually allowed their son to accompany the *qalandar*; doubtless by then Sarmad had gained more local fame, and hence was less of a stranger in his Judaeo–Islamic origins.

As Rizvi remarks, Abhai Chand seems to have been something of a prodigy, gaining proficiency in Persian and composing Persian verse, and learning to read classical Jewish literature such as the Pentateuch and the Psalms. The Persian translation of the first six chapters of *Genesis* which was incorporated in the *Dabistan* under the title of the "Book of Adam" was made by Abhai Chand; it was revised by Sarmad himself for the use of the *Dabistan* author. The *Dabistan* also incorporates a distinctive verse by Abhai Chand which states his multi-faceted affiliation with the *Quran,* the *Pentateuch,* Rabbinical Judaism, Christian monasticism, (Zoroastrian) priests, and the *kafirs* (infidels, here probably meaning Hindus).

It was in 1634–5 that Sarmad went to Lahore in the Punjab, where he became a well known figure to people from all walks of life, including high officials of the Mughal court. He was also active in Hyderabad. The Iranian merchants in Hyderabad were devoted to him; amongst these followers was Mir Muhammad Sa'id Mir Jumla (d.1663), who afterwards became a minister in the government of Hyderabad and a favourite of the emperor Aurangzeb. It does not appear to have been until 1647–8 that Sarmad met the author of the *Dabistan* at Hyderabad. Whether Sarmad had contacts prior to this with Kaivani groups at Lahore is not specified, but the chapter on Judaism in the *Dabistan* was one result of the author's collaboration with Sarmad. Fischel described Sarmad as a sufi, only superficially Islamized; Sarmad told other Jews that it was not necessary to change their religion, which may be reflective of Kaivani emphases.

It was *c.*1654 that Sarmad moved to Delhi, apparently at the invitation of Dara Shikoh. This Mughal prince was liberal in his religious views, and patronized sufis; Shikoh is well known for his efforts to mediate knowledge of the Hindu heritage amongst Muslims. Here in the Mughal capital of his father Shah Jahan, Dara Shikoh constantly visited Sarmad, and addressed him as "my master and preceptor."

The more orthodox Muslims viewed Shikoh's liberal attitudes with caution, and a hostile source (Sher Khan Lodi) writing in 1691–2 disparagingly refers to Sarmad as a lunatic. This was a common jibe of the orthodox against those with nonconformist approaches; the term *majzub* was often given the insinuation of "madman," though it actually means something quite different in sufi lore. Other "foreign" views of Sarmad were those of the European travellers Manucci and Bernier. Niccolao Manucci was a Venetian adventurer, and from 1656 served for a lengthy period as a physician at the court of Delhi and Agra. In his *Storia do Mogor* he reports that Dara Shikoh did not restrict himself to any one religion: when he was in the company of Muslims he praised Islam, when he was in the company of Jews he praised the Jewish religion, when he was with Hindus he praised Hinduism. This, adds Manucci, was the reason why Dara's brother Aurangzeb disparaged him as an infidel (*kafir*). The same source says that Dara would relish a discussion with Jesuit fathers, or to be more precise, to engage them in disputes on religion with Muslims or with "a Hebrew called Sarmad." Manucci viewed Sarmad as an atheist who went about Delhi naked, save when in courtly company, at which times he would wear a more respectable loincloth. One might add that many of the poorer Hindus wore little more than a loincloth, and that in streets where the corpses of beggars were often in view, it made relatively little difference as to whether the living were clothed from head to foot or naked as on the day of their birth.

While the Jesuits probably regarded Sarmad as an intractable Asiatic virtuoso in philosophy, the stigma of "atheism" doubtless arose owing to a misunderstanding of the apparent non-attachment to any particular belief system. Further, Sarmad doubtless offended some of the orthodox *ulama* by his composition of verses or *rubais* which ridiculed formal prayers of the divines and also "sufi" discourses by those who lacked any effective knowledge. It was thus easier to insinuate that he was a madman if one believed that one's own views comprised total sanity.

The *Dabistan* reports that Sarmad would say in defence of his appearance that the prophet Isaiah went naked during his last days. The *ulama* were not that familiar with the

Jewish prophet, and one suspects that the Jesuits viewed the statement with pious incredulity – apart from believing that there could be no more Isaiahs unless they were Christians. Amongst Hindu ascetics and yogis, the practice of nakedness was commonplace, if for no other reason than that in those days they were unable to buy apartments in Hollywood or the latest fad in silk handkerchiefs.

The diligent reader will have observed that Sarmad's sojourn at Delhi synchronizes with the completion of the *Dabistan* during the mid-1650's. The unusual format of that work clearly reveals the tactic of reviewing diverse beliefs and sects without passing a value judgment for or against (though it is evident on close inspection that the author was either a Hushangian–Kaivani or a "sufi," or both). Yet a criticism has been made of the *Dabistan* that its reporting is of a confused nature, and that even in the original Persian, it is not easy to follow its sequences and allusions. This is typical of the conservative reaction in some quarters to a liberal yet objective attitude. No wonder that the author of the *Dabistan* sometimes follows traditional cues in the non-divulgence of pearls to those who would merely cover them with manure.

Sarmad's sojourn at Delhi also coincided or synchronized with the most creative period of Dara Shikoh's literary endeavours. While many princes and nobles were merely luxuriating (in both India and Iran, and elsewhere) in the splendour of utter decadence, Dara Shikoh wrote a remarkable treatise during 1654–5 entitled *Majma al-Bahrain* (Confluence of the Two Oceans). It represents a meeting-point between the sufi and Hindu monistic traditions; ingredients for the Hindu aspect were culled from Baba Lal, who created a new sect in the tradition associated with the fifteenth century reformer Kabir.[66] Shikoh had immersed himself in seven lengthy talks with Lal at the end of 1653; Baba Lal maintained that every religion had its own "perfect saints," a perspective that was closely in harmony with Kaivani attitudes, though it can be expressed diffusely (since some religions harbour more perfect saints than others owing to "time and place" factors). Dara Shikoh was a great admirer of Kabir, and seems to have recognized the same spirit and intensity in Sarmad.

In his preface to *Majma al-Bahrain,* Shikoh writes that after being introduced to the subtleties of the intrinsic sufi tradition (his first teacher was the Qadiri shaikh Mulla Shah Badakshi), he wanted to acquaint himself with the teachings of the Hindu monists. After having repeated discussions with the latter, he did not see any difference, save in the inevitable verbal formulae of expression, in the way the two traditions sought for Truth and comprehended that Truth.

Rizvi observes that Shikoh was actually only repeating the same truth which had been relayed in different forms for the past hundred years in India concerning the essential unity of apparently disparate religio-mystical traditions. Shikoh's reconciliation of sufi and Vedantic philosophy was not new, but it was unusually dynamic and in earnest; the prince seems to have been much better informed than some other enthusiasts. His grandfather Jehangir, the Mughal emperor, had also favourably compared Vedanta to the highest form of the sufi approach, but Jehangir did not manifest the intellectual acuity of Shikoh, and he had largely modified the philosophical overtones of the Akbarian policy to suit affairs of state and leisure. If Shikoh had become the new emperor, India might have seen a greater reign even than Akbar's.

Shikoh's perspective was a little more complex than is sometimes reported. As Mahfuz-Ul-Haq observed, Shikoh's studies in Sufism led him to the conclusion that truth is not the exclusive property of any particular race, but can be discerned at all times. This conclusion was the result of a deep study and a continued association with men of different religious backgrounds and "sufis of varying opinions."[67]

Dara Shikoh had in effect connected with "high Sufism" rather than the popular varieties. Yet the perspectives of those with broader reaches of mind were always liable to contraction in the hands of imitators and shallow enthusiasts. Some of the perspectives dealt with in this chapter have become appropriated by both dogmatic and casual versions of a simplified "unity of religions" concept. The actual unity inherent in different religious formats is a very elementary matter; when plugged *ad nauseam* at the expense of finer intricacies, it is actually a testimony to the poverty of mind needing such support. The perennial philosophy may be perennial; it is also perenially attended, it would seem, by the flotsam of farthing versions of the nominal category that can be written on the back of any postage stamp.

Dara Shikoh's *Majma al-Bahrain* incorporated a chapter on *Adwar,* or the "infinity of cycles." It is commonly thought that this was due solely to the Hindu components of the treatise, but a more intensive research into the "unity of religions" might reveal further ranges in the paradigm.

In 1655–6, Shikoh sponsored a translation of the *Yoga Vashishta,* a Hindu work which had earlier been favoured by Mir Findiriski; this text receives its name from the Yoga philosophy purportedly delivered by the sage Vashishta to his royal pupil Rama. As with many Sanskrit works, neither its date nor authorship is certain.

An important literary undertaking in which Shikoh participated more closely was the Persian translation of fifty-two Upanishads in 1657. This translation was entitled *Sirr-i-Akbar* (The Great Secret), a reference to phraseology in the Upanishads, which had for long been regarded as classical treatises of philosophy by brahmins who maintained the texts in an oral format (and not in a written one, as is sometimes mistakenly assumed). The translation was carried out personally by the prince in consultation with a team of learned pundits and *sannyasins* (renunciates) of Benares. It is a monument to intercultural liaison. Though well known, it is very rarely read outside India save by a handful of specialist scholars. It was Shikoh's translation which served as a stimulant to Sanskritist studies of philosophy in Europe at a later date, though the latter trend was for the most part ignorant of the contextual situation of the precedent. Specialists nowadays like to dwell upon inaccuracies wherever these can be found; Dara Shikoh's version is not noted for its literal accuracy in intelligible Persian, but it is also very difficult to render the Upanishads accurately into modern European languages.

Shikoh wrote an introduction to his translation of the Upanishads. He briefly refers to his journey to Kashmir in 1640 where he apparently first heard of the Upanishads in any detail; this was at the time of his initial close encounter with Mulla Shah Badakshi. He says that he found unsolved mysteries in the *Quran* and the Christian Bible; he cites the *Quran* in support of his atypical contention that the Upanishads were secrets not open to all.[68]

Shikoh did not neglect in this introduction to criticize the brahmins and pundits of that day for their utter ignorance of the subtleties of monism which were easily available to them in the works of their own religion. He was here playing upon the theme of a monistic pantheism known in sufi ranks as *tauhid-i-wujudi* which could be discerned as inherent in both Islam and Hinduism, but which was commonly neglected in its essentials.

A matter of possibly even greater neglect is that of the false image of integral Indian philosophy as mediated by modern pundits and gurus of dollar idiom. The concoctions sometimes presented in both India and the West as "Yoga philosophy" and so forth are an insult to the more intelligent Hindus. What sells best is not necessarily what is most accurate. It seems that it will have to be reiterated for some while that commercial standards do not outweigh traditional warnings against the fake who thrives on popular gullibility (even if some academics are the most gullible).

It is surely too well known in history books (though one despairs of this truism sometimes) to need any restatement here that Dara Shikoh met with execution from his brother Aurangzeb in 1659. They were rivals for the Mughal throne with the oblivion of their degenerate father Shah Jahan, but their approach to matters in general was very different in each case. Dara Shikoh did not possess the military ardour necessary to defeat Aurangzeb, who was an ambitious and ruthless war leader who had the advantage of pandering to the anti-infidel sentiments of his more uninformed compatriots.

After Shikoh was beheaded in Delhi, the extent of hindsight bias can be gauged from the damnatory report of him made by the official historian Muhammad Kazim in the

Alamgir-Nama. Kazim accuses the prince of having called his "heresy" *tasawwuf* (an Arabic word for the sufi discipline), and of having been in the constant company of brahmins, yogis, and sannyasins. Nay more, the prince had regarded this "crowd of prevaricators, misguided ones and worthless fellows" as *arifs* or gnostics. Worse still perhaps, he had considered their unholy books as divine, and had committed himself to the unholy task of translating such books. If Shikoh had gained the throne, concluded Kazim, the religious law would have been in danger from infidelity and Judaism.

As it transpired, the state was in dire danger from Aurangzeb (Alamgir), who in addition to reimposing with severity the discriminatory poll-tax (*jizya*) upon Hindus, committed himself to an unproductive and lengthy war in the southernmost part of his dominion which sadly depleted the resources of the state (or rather empire), lending it substantially prone to deterioration and eventual annexation by the British.

Rizvi has observed that Shikoh's religious views were used as a political pretext in order to bolster and camouflage the political ambitions of Aurangzeb (rgd.1658–1707).[69] To Aurangzeb's credit, he detested useless luxury and himself adopted a monarchical version of the ascetic ideal, but his angle here tended to be an oppressive one for those less regally placed. Military asceticism is arguably not the ideal.

There may be much truth in the report that Aurangzeb questioned Sarmad after Shikoh's execution as to the whereabouts of the throne on which Dara was to be crowned (Sarmad is credited with having predicted that Dara would be king, though he may merely have expressed optimism on this point). Sarmad is reported to have replied: "You rule from your throne in Delhi, but Dara is enthroned in eternity."[70]

The execution of Sarmad is commonly reported as the consequence of Aurangzeb's attempt to remove Shikoh's influential supporters. But it may well be that in the case of Sarmad, it was because the latter would not acknowledge the superiority of Aurangzeb. Monarchical egotism, like other forms of the disease, has often been the cause of lethal whims and caprices.

Aurangzeb himself was not immune to sufi sentiments, and may even have admired some of the ascetic elements in the character of Sarmad. It has been inferred by some that Aurangzeb preferred the aspect of Sufism[71] which did not divulge any but the most elementary truths to those outside advanced dervish circles, in case the formal law was upset by antinomian mystics who misconstrued complex principles. There may be something to be said for this approach in its correct context, but it is a singularly convenient excuse for despotism if more advanced truths are not made available to a wider public who have a right to them, particularly if some of the truths are elementary humanitarian codes.

Sarmad probably viewed many contemporary "sufis" with a critical eye. Some of the sufi disciples of Shikoh's *murshid* Mulla Shah Badakshi are implicated as having intrigued to harm the prince, since Badakshi warned Shikoh to beware of both overt enemies and those covert ones who enrolled as his (Badakshi's) disciples. Badakshi was an atypical shaikh of the Qadiri order who had acquired a stern reputation for discouraging potential pupils, and even Shikoh himself in the beginning. He seems to have genuinely preferred a solitary and contemplative existence above all other distractions. He was also one of those who incurred Aurangzeb's displeasure, though fortunately not fatally, and he died a natural death at Lahore in 1661, and in poverty.

Sarmad's association with Shikoh further encouraged the prince in his penchant for frank mystical poetry, which had long been a medium for the more satirical expressions of diverse sufi types. In his *Diwan,* Shikoh wrote such lines as "Paradise only exists where no mulla exists." Rizvi comments that Shikoh's alienation from the *ulama* was a foregone conclusion, but does not observe that Shikoh had a good cover for his anti-mulla verses owing to the fact of his being in the shadow of Mulla Shah Badakshi, who was careful not to infringe orthodox formulations, although he himself was a *wujudi.*[72]

Sarmad may have considered that Dara Shikoh was in

need of further ranges in philosophical understanding. During his earlier years the prince had been preoccupied with notions of the all-powerful efficacy of dervish orders, but this is very much less in evidence after his encounter with Baba Lal at the end of 1653. The prince was enthusiastically inclined to ascribe himself a role of high importance in extramundane affairs, but this had not prevented a bizarre display of a traditionally mundane accompaniment to warfare in the Qandahar campaign of 1653 in which Shikoh was appointed to lead a large army against the Safavid forces. A batch of holy men were included in Shikoh's retinue, and he is reported to have ordered these *tantrikas*, yogis, and dervishes to use their magical powers against the foe.[73] The campaign was not a success; the prince was not noted for his military prowess, an attribute for which Aurangzeb has tended to be glorified, though even the orthodox Aurangzeb invoked the power of talismans during the Satnami rebellion. Shikoh was no better than Aurangzeb in this respect therefore, though such practices appear to have been traditional in India since the time of the *Atharva Veda*. For believers in the power of karma, it seems strange that those concerned should have ignored the warning that the aggressive use of magic will rebound upon the practitioner with a greater force than he himself aims in the first instance. One of the yogis in Shikoh's Qandahar entourage might well have reflected upon this irony when he was captured by the Safavid soldiers and commanded to work his magic against his own army; his magic failed however, and he was afterwards hurled to his death from the walls of the fort of Qandahar.

Whatever the deficiencies in his background of peacock thrones and jewel-studded swords, Shikoh appears to have been at his most mature peak in his "Confluence" and his introduction to the Upanishads (or rather Upnikhats to borrow a Muslim term of reference). He was perhaps ingenious with an almost Sarmadic inflection in accusing brahmin pundits of concealing the Upanishads from Muslims in their attempt to conceal the subtleties of the *Tauhid* which these venerable treatises contained. He also chided the pundits for having withheld these texts from a large number of unprivileged Hindus who were consequently unaware of Upanishadic philosophy. He did not neglect to maintain, in a more orthodox style, that his translation was intended to elucidate the *Quran*.[74]

The Latin version of the "Oupnekhat" by the French scholar Duperron was published in 1801–2. Scholars have since deemed this translation to be barbarous, but the dour Schopenhauer was one of those fascinated by the contents, to the extent that he wrote in his *Die Welt als Wille und Vorstellung*: "In the whole world there is no study, except that of the originals, so beneficial and so elevating as that of the *Oupnekhat*." He nevertheless misunderstood the contents, possibly because of the Latin translation, or perhaps owing to the truncated interpretation of Hinayana Buddhism then in vogue, or conceivably because neo-Kantian philosophers still had a long way to go before grasping the meaning of life. In fairness to Schopenhauer however, his realism was a refreshing change from Hegelian elitism. Kant passed a favourable verdict upon the Hindus, and his theory of the thing-in-itself has been deemed similar by some commentators to Upanishadic concepts, though it may be that transcendentalism could have more usefully learnt a thing or two from Islamic and Hindu sectors if studies had been less influenced by Christian morality. By comparison, Marx became more historical in delving into Indian history, but in actual fact he was only studying colonialized reports from which he sought to establish proof for his preconceived thesis of an aggressive and violent philosophy.

It was Manucci who reported that after Shikoh's execution, Aurangzeb commanded that Sarmad be brought to his presence. In reply to the new monarch's question as to the whereabouts of his devoted patron, Sarmad replied that Dara still lived, but that he was invisible to Aurangzeb, since Aurangzeb had tyrannized those of his own blood, and in his ambition to usurp the kingdom he had taken the life of his brother and perpetrated other barbarities. The response of the wrathful monarch was to order that Sarmad should be beheaded.

Manucci's anecdotes are not always totally reliable specimens of history, and it is probable that we have here only the barest outline of what actually occurred. The *Dabistan* was finished prior to Sarmad's demise, and the later reports by Muslim authors are fragmentary and embellished with legendary elements. Nevertheless, it is apparent that Sarmad faced a formidable hostility from the divines in elite positions, in addition to whatever personal feelings of pique Aurangzeb may have nurtured.

The report by Shah Nawaz Khan in the *Maasir al-Umara* says that Aurangzeb sent Itimad Khan Mulla Abdul Qawi to persuade Sarmad to desist from his practice of nudity. Sarmad would not acquiesce to this pressure, and sarcastically retorted, using a play on words: "Satan is *Qawi* (powerful)." Mulla Qawi's ego was apparently offended by the response, and he seems to have reported very adversely against the jiber.

This anecdote occurs in a biography of Mulla Qawi, which depicts him as being proud and ostentatious owing to his position of royal tutor and *Qazi-ul-Quzzat* (chief *qazi* or legist). Basking in imperial patronage of the more zealous kind, Qawi's conceit was lent fuel by his knowledge of law and theology, owing to which he took a very biased view of matters outside his department. (Qawi died the victim of a Turkish sword in 1666–7, a detail which the writer of his biography appears to have found significant). It was this mentality of orthodox mullas against which men like Sarmad and Dara Shikoh were struggling. It may be ironic that Sarmad is sometimes called Mulla Sarmad; the fact that he was well-versed in Arabic philosophy and science apparently meant little to those who adhered only to the Arabic letter of the law.

Sarmad was executed on pretexts contrived by Aurangzeb or the *qazis*, or more likely by both. It seems that Sarmad categorically refused the order of the court to wear clothes, though this more probably entailed a complete recanting of his attitudes and allegiances. Aurangzeb is said to have argued with the *ulama* that nobody could be executed with any justification merely for being undressed. A more conglomerate charge was therefore advanced against the heretic for being a partisan of the heretical Dara Shikoh, as one who did not believe in the literal bodily ascent (*miraj*) of the Prophet Muhammad to the heavens, and as one who furthermore went naked and denied the existence of God because he had not had any personal knowledge of God. If the last clause is at all accurate (following Hashmi), then it is likely to have been a distortion of the sufi standpoint that those lacking personal knowledge of what they declaim are an effective denial of divine prerogative, i.e., mullas and pundits dependent upon the letter and not the spirit.

Sarmad was executed in Delhi in 1660–1.[75] By that time it is probably true to say that he had had his fill of seeing pompous and lavishly bedecked theologians and noblemen, some with bejewelled turbans, some with jewel-encrusted daggers in their belts, and some with dogmatic voices who knew no path to reason or intuition and nor compassion. Many of them wore clothes that cost more per head than a team of craftsmen were able to earn in months of toil on such monuments as the Taj Mahal.

The transit from oppression to freedom may not always be a geographical one, though Sarmad evidently possessed sufficient complexity of thought not to simplistically correlate life after death with any ultimate mode of travel; the section on Judaism in the *Dabistan* reflects Sarmad's *tanasukh* perspective, though in an abbreviated form which it would be unwise to interpret literally.

It is reported that when Sarmad was being led to the place of execution, he was uttering extempore quatrains amongst the dense crowd of spectators. The executioner was a low caste man, a sweeper (which, if accurate, means an untouchable). According to the custom for these fatal occasions, the executioner made to cover the victim's head in preparation for decapitation. But Sarmad indicated that this was not necessary, and remarked:

> "The friend with the naked sword has come.
> In whatever guise You come I recognize You."[76]

This couplet might be taken as an illustration of the psychological stance adopted by the Advaita Vedanta, which levels all distinctions between rich and poor, male and female, colour and creed, and so forth. It does not, however, advocate the Nietzchean version of going "beyond good and evil," which in the contemporary West has led to anomalies of nihilism and misconduct such as are equivalent to the tantric and related practices of ritual murder and similar misfortunes.

It is evident from the reliable testimony of the *Dabistan* that Sarmad composed "good verses." Sarmad was in fact his pen-name, as he was otherwise known as Muhammad Sa'id. Of the many quatrains (*rubaiyat*) attributed to Sarmad, Hashmi remarked that he had no definitive criterion by which to attribute authorship of any one quatrain to Sarmad. But he did attribute to Sarmad the lines: "I am not a follower of the thought and ways of any trend, but in *ghazal* I follow the style of Hafiz, and in *rubai* I am a disciple of Khayaam – though I do not sip for long at his wine-cup either."[77]

Though Hashmi remarked that he could not hazard a guess as to the agency which preserved the Sarmadian quatrains, individuals like Abhai Chand and Mobad Shah are unlikely to have forgotten the execution in a hurry, and doubtless did their best to preserve what they could. Sarmad was not forgotten at popular level, since he soon became a legendary figure, and eventually acquired a respectable status in Muslim annals. It is perhaps apt enough that he achieved the same rank in popular estimation that Hallaj possessed, and hence duplicating the achievement of Sohravardi Maqtul.

It is difficult to say how quickly popular feeling about Sarmad's execution made itself felt at the court, but Rizvi has feasibly suggested that these popular sentiments contributed to the sudden change in Aurangzeb's attitude to Nimatullah Qadiri of Narnaul (d.1666–7), a sufi saint of strong pantheist tendencies and humanitarian disposition who had settled in distant Bengal. It was perhaps a worried and diplomatic Aurangzeb who began to write letters on intricate points of sufi lore to Nimatullah shortly after 1660.

Aurangzeb undoubtedly respected the sufi phenomenon according to his own lights, in forms and doses amenable to him. Even while leaving for the north to fight his brother Dara Shikoh, this stern warrior had craved for the blessings of Shaikh Burhan Shattari (d.1678) of Burhanpur, one of the most prominent sufi leaders of the time, and one who notably could number among his followers people of diverse castes and creeds. Burhan was well known for his dislike of personal visits to rulers, and the lordly Aurangzeb was even prepared to approach him at night *incognito,* sitting in the common crowd. But it was only with reluctance that Shaikh Burhan consented to see him at the persuasion of some comrades; the name of Aurangzeb evidently did not inspire him with enthusiasm for a *tête-à-tête,* and his attitude was that if Aurangzeb came to his *khanaqah* (retreat), then he (Burhan) would leave. The prince complained to him that Dara Shikoh was lax in matters of religious form, and that he (Aurangzeb) would enforce the religious law and see to the welfare of the people. Burhan's reply was brief and impartial, reiterating that the prince should do justice and cherish his subjects. But what could the blessings of poor dervishes do for a king?[78]

If Aurangzeb found it difficult to win the approval of certain of the more rigorous ascetic figureheads of that time, it is arguable that his version of asceticism was an extreme form of literalism in non-alignment with the more comprehensive ascetic disposition that was also in evidence. Moral censorship (*ihtisab*) may have been indulgently amoral in creating a vested interest amongst the bureaucracy, which gained a source of legal income from 1679 onwards via the reimposition of the *jizya* upon Aurangzeb's Hindu subjects in order to maintain the officials of the censorship department.

It is now more apparent than formerly that the *wujudi* pantheists of expansive inter-religious views continued to exert a considerable influence during the lengthy reign of Aurangzeb. One manifestation which the latter monarch very nearly obliterated was the treatise known as *Taswiyah,* written by Shaikh Muhibbullah Mubariz Ilahabadi (d.1648). Muhibbullah was a member of the Chishti order of dervishes, and resided in Allahabad for the last twenty years of his life, where he set about popularizing the works of Ibn al-Arabi. According to Rizvi, Muhibbullah's versions possess no originality, though the short treatise in Arabic known as *Taswiyah* was impactive as a vehicle for the concepts promulgated by the Spanish Arab of Murcia. This *wujudi* treatise includes such assertions as: the angels were spiritual forces and not entities as commonly conceived; the archangel Gabriel was within the Prophet Muhammad and not external to him; Satan (Shaitan) was within each person, and all discord within the personality and psychology was a consequence of personal deficit, which produced such far-reaching problems, though the question of duality does not intrinsically arise, since tranquillity can also be evoked by personal orientation.

Aurangzeb is reported to have reacted strongly against the *Taswiyah*, but this is thought to have been mainly owing to Muhibbullah's close contact with Dara Shikoh; Rizvi observes that Aurangzeb could not have failed to know that there was nothing new in this treatise, which was a basic variant of Arabi's *Fusus al-Hikam*. By the time of royal displeasure, Muhibbullah was dead and gone, but Aurangzeb learnt that two of his pupils were in the capital – namely Mir Sayed Muhammad Qannauji, who was an imperial servant (i.e. official), and one Shaikh Muhammadi, who led the retired life of an ascetic. When Qannauji was asked to give an explanation for the unorthodox contents of the stigmatized treatise, he tactfully denied ever having been a disciple of Muhibbullah. An imperial despatch was then sent to the aloof Shaikh Muhammadi, declaring that if he claimed to be a disciple he should reconcile the *Taswiyah* with the religious law, but that if incapable of doing this, then he should express repentance for his discipleship to the heretic and burn all copies of the obnoxious treatise. With a not inconsiderable courage, Shaikh Muhammadi sent back a reply that he did not deny having been a disciple of Muhibbullah, but that he was not repentant of this fact, since he had not himself achieved the more advanced state of mind from which Muhibbullah had talked; furthermore, more fire was available in the royal kitchen than in the dwellings of ascetics. Muhammadi was, however, suitably subservient in adding that orders could be issued to burn any copies of the treatise that could be found. Aurangzeb appears to have felt that he had crushed the opposition, unless he had thought better of arousing unnecessary popular feelings, for he thereafter remained quiet on the subject and did not even restrict study of the *Taswiyah*.

There may have been further reason for suspicion attaching to Shaikh Muhammadi in that he had undertaken a systematic study of Hindu mysticism and philosophy with Hindu pundits. But Aurangzeb could do little against this if those concerned acknowledged royal wishes. Muhibbullah himself had emphasized the acquisition of knowledge from the Hindus, and in one of his letters quoted the Hindu theory of cosmogony, though Rizvi says that his knowledge of Hinduism appears to have been "very superficial."[79]

Another disciple of Shaikh Muhibbullah was Muhsin Fani (d.1670), who, as Schimmel remarks, was for long credited with authorship of the *Dabistan,* though that book seems to have been written by a Parsi author. Fani was another of those connected with Dara Shikoh, and during the latter part of his life was based in Kashmir where Shikoh and other members of the Mughal court were in the habit of spending many of their summers.[80] Fani wrote Persian poetry, specimens of which are quoted in the *Dabistan,* and hence giving rise to the confusion over authorship.

Rizvi concluded a major study by stating that whatever was achieved in terms of an effective revitalization of the Muslim society of Aurangzeb's reign and the reigns of his Mughal successors was the outcome of contributions from the supporters of *wahdat al-wujud* (unity of being) and the concomitant attitude of "peace with all." This school of thought had a wider appeal in India than in any other zone of the Islamic world; its marked popularity during the reign of the puritannical Aurangzeb was its greatest victory. The *wujudi* spirit continued to inspire all sections of the North Indian population until the mid-nineteenth century when new influences were unleashed owing to the imperialistic schemes of the British.[81]

This data has for long been obscured in Indian annals and neglected by sociologists and others. Even the term *wahdat al-wujud* tends to be mistranslated in standard works.[82] Though commonly associated with the teachings of Ibn al-Arabi, the *wujudi* tradition was extremely diverse and often original – though there were also a mort of mediocre and even banal copyists.

When Sir William Jones (1746–94) landed at Calcutta in 1783, it was, to use Troyer's words, with ideas of "vast projects, embracing, with the extension of science, the general improvement of mankind." Jones was an exceptional scholar, and one suspects that he frequently puzzled his compatriots in his enthusiasm for research into the linguistic and other complexities of the Indians, Arabs, Tartars, Persians, and Chinese. The coffers of the East India Company had for long been swelling, and in general there was a distinct lack of empathy with what was going on amongst the natives. Thugs and fanatics apart, India's status was that of a mere moonstone for most of the convenience with which it was approached and glossed.

When Jones made such observations as "when the learner is able to understand the images and allusions in the Persian poems, he will see a reason in every line why they cannot be translated literally into any European language,"[83] this meant only an excuse for not studying non-European languages and their idioms for those who were too busy with getting on in the world at everyone else's expense.

In 1787 Jones read through a lengthy Persian manuscript which he had obtained from Mir Muhammad Hussein, whom Lord Teignmouth described as "one of the most intelligent Muselmans in India." In June of that year, Jones wrote enthusiastically of this document to the future Lord Teignmouth, saying that it contained "more recondite learning, more entertaining history, more beautiful specimens of poetry, more ingenuity and wit," and more blasphemy, than he had ever seen amassed in a single volume.[84] In brief, Sir William Jones had discovered the *Dabistan*.

Though it was subsequently discovered that other manuscript copies of the *Dabistan* were in the possession of the Nawab of Oudh and Dastur Mulla Firuz of Bombay, this assortment of manuscripts does not mitigate the looming factor of how much of the contextual data is missing. An interesting and possibly highly relevant sidelight to this is afforded by the tangible instance of a treatise which appeared even before the Persian text of the *Dabistan* could be printed in 1789 in the *New Asiatic Miscellany*.[85] I am referring to the Gujerati book entitled *Mukulat-i-Bahmani* which was published in 1788. It was written by Dastur Mulla Kaus bin Rustom, the father of Mulla Firuz, and the man who found the surviving manuscript of the *Desatir* in Iran. This Kaivani-style work refers to Azar Kaivan as having visited Agra, Patna and Kashmir during the 1560's in Akbar's reign. The later Parsi scholar Jivanji J. Modi clearly deemed this work to contain errors or embellishments, which may well be true, though the chronology of Kaivan's arrival in India may be no more erroneous than Modi's preferred late date of the early 1580's, which is very conjectural and not at all definitive.[86] Suffice it to say that if Azar Kaivan arrived at Agra by 1575, then this factor alone could be of potent significance for certain impulses manifest in Akbar's lengthy reign.

With regard to this conjectural time and place, it is relevant to observe that Akbar's new city of Fatehpur Sikri was built at a site some twenty miles from Agra, founded in 1568 and where construction work continued until 1585, at which time it was abandoned. It has what is comparable to the reputation of an Amarna insofar as tradition and innovation are concerned. In 1575 the Ibadat Khana (House of Worship) was established in this royal settlement, where representatives of different religions and sects could meet and debate. Abu'l Fazl wrote in the *Akbar-Nama* that (minus the hyperbole) a proclamation was issued inviting all orders and sects to assemble in the precincts – "those who searched after spiritual and physical truth, and those of the common public who sought for an awakening."[87] It was this feature, and not so much the Hindu architectural styles, that made Fatehpur Sikri an intellectual and philosophical landmark of that era.

Akbar had first met Europeans in 1572 during the campaign in Gujerat, and he began to seriously investigate the Parsis at Surat in 1573, though it was not until the late 1570's that he invited the Navsari priests and a Jesuit mission from Goa to his new capital. He did not establish the new order of *din-i-ilahi* until 1582, though he had abolished the *jizya* nearly twenty years earlier. His tactic of appointing the warrior-like Rajputs to high positions has been viewed as part of a successful project of expansionism that continued until 1600 to integrate widespread areas of the Indian subcontinent into his empire. While the military successes of Akbar cannot be denied even by partisans of his liberality, it remains a fact that Rajputs were Hindus, and that Akbar had prohibited the enslavement of Hindu prisoners of war in addition to the crippling poll-tax.

Akbar accumulated an extensive library that has often impressed connoisseurs by its variety. Its contents included books on natural history, anthropology, medicine, astronomy, mathematics, engineering, classics, and translations of religious works. It is most unlikely that Akbar himself read any of these books, since he was illiterate – though he was an accomplished conversationalist and was evidently very partial to finely illustrated volumes. Some of the men in his entourage were very literate however, and it is probably they who were ultimately responsible for some of the memorable Akbarian developments.

It was in 1575 that Abu'l Fazl Allami, then still in his mid-twenties, presented himself to Akbar for the second time. Yet he writes that he was weary of seeing men of his own country, and that he had no inclination for society; he did not think it right to embark upon a career in the world without the permission of his father, Shaikh Mubarak Nagauri.[88] Abu'l Fazl was here describing the transition from his more contemplative existence to royal favour; the former is not well understood in some accounts, though important since Abu'l Fazl gained high esteem from Akbar owing to his scholarly criticism of the narrow-minded *ulama* in the discussions associated with the Ibadat Khana. It was therefore in 1575, or at a date soon following, that Akbar appears to have been most susceptible to above average currents of thought, even in comparatively small doses that may have been transmitted through slight personal contact, or even conceivably at second hand.

If there is in fact a valid question-mark with respect to time and place extensions of the life and influence of Azar Kaivan, then this might be considered strangely apt in view of the longer term uncertainties of time and place complexities attendant upon Zarathushtra,[89] the founder of the tradition with which Kaivan is chiefly associated – or to be more precise, the complexities attendant upon one of the figureheads honoured by the prophetology of Kaivan's tradition.

NOTES TO PART TWO

1. J.J. Modi, "The Parsees at the Court of Akbar and Dastur Meherji Rana," *Journal of the Bombay Branch of the Royal Asiatic Society* (Bombay 1904) 21: 69–245, p. 99.
2. M. Boyce, *Zoroastrians: Their Religious Beliefs and Practices* (London: Routledge & Kegan Paul, 1979), p. 183.
3. M. Mujeeb, *The Indian Muslims* (London: George Allen & Unwin, 1967), pp. 261–3.
4. J.J. Modi, "A Parsee High Priest (Dastur Azar Kaiwan, 1529–1614 A.D.) with his Zoroastrian disciples in Patna, in the 16th and 17th Century A.C.," *Jnl of the K.R. Cama Oriental Institute* (Bombay 1932), 20: 1–85, pp. 25 ff.
5. It is apparent that Modi's preferred late dating for Kaivan's arrival in India could have been influenced by his view that it was the Indian Parsis, and not the Irani Zoroastrians, who had inspired Akbar's interest in Zoroastrian ideas. See Modi, 1904 *art. cit.,* pp. 153–4. It is therefore not impossible that Kaivan arrived in India substantially earlier than 1581, and that he did have some impact upon Akbar's thinking, however slight.
6. S.H. Nasr, "The School of Ispahan" (904–932) in M.M. Sharif, ed., *A History of Muslim Philosophy Vol. 2* (Wiesbaden: Otto Harrassowitz, 1966), pp. 909 ff.
7. D. Shea and A. Troyer, trans., *The Dabistan or School of Manners Vol. 1* (Paris, 1843), pp. 140–1.
8. S.H. Nasr, *Sadr al-Din Shirazi and his Transcendent Theosophy* (Tehran: Iranian Academy of Philosophy, 1978), p. 34.
9. S.H. Nasr, "The School of Ispahan," pp. 922 ff.
10. Cf. Modi, 1932 *art. cit.,* pp. 26, 31.
11. M. Mujeeb, *op. cit.,* p. 261, citing Badauni.
12. Shea and Troyer trans., Vol. 1, pp. 102–3.
13. *Ibid.,* p. 103.

14. *Ibid.*, p. 142.
15. Modi, 1932 *art. cit.*, pp. 25 ff.
16. Modi, *art. cit.*, pp. 63 ff.
17. See my *Minds and Sociocultures,* Appendix.
18. Modi, *art. cit.*, p. 6.
19. P. Spear, *A History of India Vol. 2* (Harmondsworth: Penguin, 1970), pp. 36–7, Cf. S.A.A. Rizvi, *A Religious and Intellectual History of the Muslims in Akbar's Reign,* with special reference to Abu'l Fazl (New Delhi: Munshiram Manoharlal, 1975).
20. A. Schimmel, *Islam in the Indian Subcontinent* (Leiden: E.J. Brill, *Handbuch der Orientalistik,* 1980), pp. 79 ff., stating that among the nineteen members of Abu'l Fazl's circle, only one was a Hindu.

For the best English translation of the *Mahabharata,* see J.A.B. Van Buitenen, trans., *The Mahabharata* (University of Chicago Press, 1973—multi-volume project). As Buitenen remarks in his intro. to Vol. 1, the Akbar-sponsored translation of the *Mahabharata* was a complete one.

21. H. Corbin, *Spiritual Body and Celestial Earth: From Mazdean Iran to Shi'ite Iran,* trans. N. Pearson (Princeton University Press, 1977), pp. 13–14. The amesha-spentas (amahraspands) are sometimes translated as "archangels," while the yazatas or *izads* are "angels" in comparative stature (Cf. *ibid.*, p. 9). On the amesha-spentas, see my *Minds and Sociocultures,* Part Two.

The meaning of the Avestan form of *khvarenah* is not agreed upon by all experts. See, e.g., H.W. Bailey, *Zoroastrian Problems in the Ninth Century Books* (Oxford: Clarendon Press, repr. with new introduction, 1971), pp. 1 ff. for a lengthy treatment and analysis of *khvarenah* and its later variants. See particularly the new introduction, pp. xvi ff. Bailey prefers "fortune" as a translation from the Achaemenid era onwards, though stating that it can be paraphrased by "glory" or "majesty." Cf. G. Gnoli, *Zoroaster's Time and Homeland* (Naples: Istituto Universitario Orientale, 1980), pp. 195–6 n. 71, who accuses Bailey of not taking into account recent researches, and who considers Bailey's theory of the evolution of *khvarenah* as "quite unlikely." Gnoli is supporting the connection of *khvarenah* with the notions of luminous strength and splendour, which according to Bailey are secondary overtones.

22. H. Corbin, *The Man of Light in Iranian Sufism,* trans. N. Pearson (Boulder, Colorado: Shambhala, 1978), p. 138.
23. G. Gnoli, op. cit., pp. 195–6.
24. M. Boyce, *Zoroastrians* (1979), p. 10, referring to the ancient divinity Khvarenah, associated with Mithra and Apam Napat.
25. Cf. Shea and Troyer trans., Vol. 3, p. 139; Vol. 1, p. 87.
26. S.H. Nasr, *An Introduction to Islamic Cosmological Doctrines* (revised edn, London: Thames and Hudson, 1978), pp. 185–6.
27. Modi, *art. cit.,* p. 66.
28. *Ibid.,* p. 7 n. 2.
29. *Ibid.,* p. 49.
30. Cf. *ibid.,* pp. 34 ff.
31. There is no mention of a successor in the *Dabistan,* though it seems that some later writers may have thought that Kaivan's "son," Khaikhushru ibn Kaivan, was a successor, owing to a mistaken extrapolation from the *Jam-i-Khaikhushru.*
32. At the time when Modi wrote his article on the Kaivanis, he only knew of the Gujerati version of the *Sharistan,* published in 1854 in Bombay. The translator was Dastur Edalji Darabji Rustomji Sanjana, an elderly high priest, who affirmed that the fourth *chaman* did not exist, though it was said to have treated of Kaivan and his ancestors. Dastur Edalji related that he had heard from his grandfather Rustomji (a learned dastur) that the *Dabistan* itself formed the fourth *chaman.* It was this data which led Modi to the debatable conclusion that the elder Behram was the author of the *Dabistan,* despite the report of this individual in the third person (Modi, *art. cit.,* pp. 21 ff.).

In a postscript to his article, Modi added that he had only heard at proof stage of the existence of the 1862–3 published edition of the *Sharistan,* the Persian text of which did incorporate a fourth *chaman.* Modi cautiously urged that this fourth *chaman* should be carefully examined before accepting it as an integral part of the work (*art. cit.,* pp. 84–5). Cf. H. Corbin, *En Islam Iranien,* Vol. 2 (Paris: Gallimard, 1971), p. 357 n. 503, who summarizes the 1862–3 edition as containing in respect of the four *chamans*: (i) a description of the cycle of prophets, including Hushang (ii) a treatment of the Kayanian heroes of Iran and Zarathushtra (iii) the Arsacids and Sassanians (iv) cosmography and geography. The second *chaman* is by far the longest, consisting of several hundred pages, with pronounced ishraqi ingredients. Corbin's treatment is extremely brief, and the *Sharistan* arguably deserves more attention than it has hitherto received. Cf. C.A. Storey, *Persian Literature: a Bio-bibliographical Survey, Vol. 1 Part 1* (London: Luzac, 1927–39), pp. 245–6, who reports the 1909 edition as "apparently complete," and who refers to the bibliographical note earlier quoted by Rieu which informs that the *Sharistan* was written in the time of Akbar.

33. S.H. Nasr, "The Spread of the Illuminationist School of Suhrawardi," *Islamic Quarterly* (1970) 14: 111–121, pp. 115–16.

34. This was a village about an hour's journey north of the ancient site of Persepolis, and in the near vicinity of several other sites of ancient monuments. Though Istakhar had become a virtually extinct cultural centre, it had once been the religious centre and the official capital of the Sassanians; it appears to have been founded soon after the decline of the Achaemenid centre of Persepolis, the ruins of which formed a quarry for the new town. It was still an important town in the early Islamic era, but by the twelfth century A.D. had dwindled to the size of a modest village with no more than about a hundred inhabitants. See M. Streck–G.C. Miles, "Istakhr" (219–222) in *The Encyclopaedia of Islam*, Vol. 4 (new edn, Leiden: E.J. Brill, 1978).

It may be that the name of Istakhar in the *Dabistan* represents an approximation of Kaivan's place of abode. He may have lived in some isolated retreat in this historic locale, which is some distance from Shiraz.

35. Cf. M. Eliade, "Some Notes on *Theosophia perennis*: Ananda K. Coomaraswamy and Henry Corbin," *History of Religions* (1979) 19(2): 167–176. The theories of Coomaraswamy do not meet with total agreement from other scholars (cf. my *The Resurrection of Philosophy,* chapter nine). Eliade describes how Corbin wanted to establish a new type of university in rebellion against what he considered to be the reductionist fallacies of "scientism," "historicism," and "sociologism," but incorporating a thorough scholarly preparation. Corbin did in fact found such an institution in France in 1974, but limited investigations to the three "Religions of the Book," i.e., Islam, Christianity, and Judaism. Eliade rather mildly criticizes this feature: "one regrets the absence of Indian and other Asiatic religions." (pp. 173–4). Cf. S.H. Nasr, *Sufi Essays* (London: George Allen & Unwin, 1972), p. 111, who urges that Islam receives the least satisfactory

treatment from those interested in comparative religion. I agree that phenomenology has not been sufficient to remedy the situation, but disagree that it has provided an improvement over the historical method.

36. See K. Ch'en, *Buddhism in China: A Historical Survey* (Princeton University Press, 1964), pp. 437 ff, 443 ff. See also Chun-fang Yu, *The Renewal of Buddhism in China: Chu-hung and the Late Ming Synthesis* (New York: Columbia University Press, 1981).

37. Modi, *art. cit.,* p. 45 n. 4, inferring that *tapreh* was here Indianized, since the word has less relevant connotations in Persian.

38. M. Eliade, *A History of Religious Ideas Vol. 1,* trans. W.R. Trask (London: Collins, 1979), p. 233. Though correct enough in this basic perspective, Eliade fails to qualitatively distinguish between the various manifestations of *tapas,* e.g., fasting, the absorption of intoxicating substances. The last-mentioned is not considered an authentic manifestation by several traditions.

39. The treatise known as *Kheshtab* has been variously stated to be a translation by Mobad Sarosh of a Sassanian work, and a translation by Mobad Hosh (or his son). The latter appears to have been a pupil in the Kaivan school, though he is not mentioned in the collective list of disciples in the *Dabistan*. The author of this extant treatise defines the word *kheshtab* as meaning "self-burning," in reference to the name of a Zoroastrian fire temple and its perpetual sacred fire. This symbolic interpretation could have more in common with the original context of sacred fires than orthodox ritual versions. "Self-burning" might more accurately fit the conflagration of the ego-nature that asserts itself in many entities, including would-be gurus. However, the *Kheshtab* treatise concerns itself primarily with nearly fifty arguments asserting the existence of the Absolute. While Modi focussed upon the 1848 publication of a Gujerati translation by Mobad Dosabhai S. Munshi, the *Kheshtab* treatise was also included in the composite work *Ayin-i Hushang* published in Bombay in 1879, in which Mirza Bahram Rustom Nasrabadi also included the Persian work *Zindeh-Rud* by Mobad Khushi, the *Risala-i Zardusht Afshar* by Mobad Sarosh, and the even less well known *Zurah,* which is another Pahlavi-style treatise. Cf. *Ayin-i*

Hushang, ed. with introduction (in Persian) by Manekji Limji Hushang Hataria (Tehran, A.H. 1295–6; C.U.L. cat. no. S828 b. 87. 8). Hataria was a Parsi who resided at Tehran on behalf of the Society for the Amelioration of the Conditions of the Zoroastrians in Persia. He was chiefly responsible for the growth of the Zoroastrian colony at Tehran. Originally a small-time merchant, he was also known as Dervish Fani.

The four treatises above-mentioned were all said to be translations into Persian from the Pahlavi. *Zardusht-Afshar,* described as a treatise on man, was attributed to the ancient entity Hakim Hushguy; *Zindeh-Rud,* a treatise on immortality, was attributed to Zindah Azaram; the *Zurah* treatise, on the subject of ethics, was attributed to Azarpazhuh, though purportedly derived from the words of Anushirvan.

40. A *sadhaka* is one who performs *sadhana,* a Sanskrit word which has acquired some rather distorted meanings in India, particularly in relation to Hindu Tantric rites. Often a short-term basis is adopted for cheap benefits, much in the manner of a stunt for publicity purposes. McLeod gave an excellent definition of *sadhana* as "method of attaining or 'realizing' an ultimate spiritual objective." See W.H. McLeod, *Guru Nanak and the Sikh Religion* (Delhi: Oxford University Press, 1976), p. 244. In Tibet the word was translated and assumed a meaning relating to the evocation of deities, for which the non-phonetic transliteration is *sgrub thabs*. See A. Wayman, *The Buddhist Tantras* (New York: Samuel Weiser, 1973), p. 54.

41. E.g., several Western commentators have followed Troyer's translation (following Gladwin) as "The School of Manners," but according to Sayed Idries Shah al-Hashimi, a more correct rendition of *Dabistan* is "The Abode of Pomp." See *The Religion of the Sufis* (London: Octagon Press, 1979), p. 6.

42. M. Boyce, *Zoroastrians* (1979), pp. 97–8, 65.

43. This information comes from a marginal note to the manuscript owned by Mulla Firuz in Bombay. Erskine notably inclined to the view that Mobad Shah was the author of the *Dabistan*. The marginal note refers to this Mobad Shah as Amir Zulfikar Ali-al-Husaini, along with typical overtones of a styled context reflecting ancient pre-Islamic Iranian associations, e.g., "the imperial Anushirvan," who appears in the *Zurah* treatise. Troyer nevertheless disregarded the view of both Erskine and Mulla

Firuz, and continued to call the author by the presumed name of Muhsin Fani. See the Preliminary Discourse in Shea and Troyer's translation, Vol. 1. Cf. C. Rieu, *Catalogue of the Persian Manuscripts in the British Museum Vol. 1* (London 1879), pp. 141–3, who was already stating that the English version of the *Dabistan* cannot be depended upon for accuracy. In addition to the Mulla Firuz manuscript, Rieu informs that Mobad Shah is named as the author in one of the British Museum copies of the *Dabistan*, and in a manuscript mentioned by Sir William Ouseley in his *Travels*. In another BM copy, Mulla Muhammad Amin is named as the author; this last manuscript is dated A.H. 1206 (A.D. 1792), a typically late date of transcription. Rieu was of the view that Mobad was the poetical designation (*takhallus*) of the author, and clearly thought that the writer concerned was a Zoroastrian. He pointed out that this writer's glowing account of the Kaivanis (=Sipasis =Abadis) presents a marked contrast to his description of Islamism (*sic*), which is that of "a well-informed outsider, not of a born and bred Muslim." Rieu says that the *Dabistan* author was born in Patna, and corrects the Shea and Troyer trans. in its erroneous reading of the author being torn away from the shores of Persia, which is rendered by Rieu as "fortune tore him away from his Parsi surroundings" in order to make him the associate of Hindus. Rieu's overall conclusion was that the *Dabistan* was written "in perfect harmony with the principles of enlightened toleration which . . . . characterized that remarkable community," here meaning the Kaivanis.

In the later history of cataloguing, Ivanow affirmed that the name of the *Dabistan* author was still not precisely known; the colophon of his twelfth century A.H. copy gave the author's name as Dhu'l-Fiqar Beg, with the *takhallus* of Muayyad (but which might represent Mobad). See W. Ivanow, *Concise Descriptive Catalogue of the Persian Manuscripts in the Collection of the Asiatic Society of Bengal* (Calcutta 1924), pp. 544–5. Cf. V.D.B. Taraporevala and D.N. Marshall, *Mughal Bibliography: Select Persian Sources for the study of Mughals in India* (Bombay: New Book Co. Private Ltd, 1962), pp. 100–1, which unequivocally catalogues the *Dabistan* under the name of Mobad Shah, adding that in the colophons of several manuscripts the book is attributed to Mir Zulfaqar Ali al-Husayni, whose *takhallus* was Mobad Shah.

44. According to Modi, Chatur Vapah belonged to the "Nagar

Brahmins," and Shea and Troyer were wrong in rendering Nagar as Naga in their Vol. 2. However, Modi neglected to bring out the full flavour of the contact (cf. Modi, *art. cit.*, p. 9).

45. R. Thapar, *A History of India Vol. 1* (Harmondsworth: Penguin, 1966), p. 20, appropriately observing that the chanting of the *gayatri* verse has a history of some three millenia, though the context in which it is chanted today cannot be said to have remained unchanged; further, it is a matter of surprise that while nineteenth century European scholarship acutely stressed the discovery of evolutionary patterns in European history, the same approach was never applied to the study of Asian history. Interesting information collected during the nineteenth century on Indian society and religion was rarely integrated into standard historical works (*ibid.*). One might add that the informational heritage is still largely unintegrated even with regard to nineteenth century developments, let alone earlier phenomena such as the Kaivani groups of the Mughal era.

46. F. Whaling, *The Rise of the Religious Significance of Rama* (Delhi: Motilal Banarssidas, 1980), pp. 221 ff.

47. J.T.F. Jordens, "Medieval Hindu Devotionalism" (266–280) in A.L. Basham, ed., *A Cultural History of India* (Oxford: Clarendon Press, 1975), p. 276.

48. Cf. Modi, *art. cit.*, pp. 47–8.

49. On Nurbakhsh, see J. Spencer Trimingham, *The Sufi Orders in Islam* (Oxford: Clarendon Press, 1971), pp. 57, 102. Cf. S.A.A. Rizvi, *A History of Sufism in India Vol. 1* (New Delhi: Munshiram Manoharlal, 1978), pp. 298–9. See also A.Q. Rafiqi, *Sufism in Kashmir from the Fourteenth to the Sixteenth Century* (Delhi: Bharatiya Publishing House, n.d., Australian National University Thesis 1972), p. 97, informing that Sayed Mhd Nurbakhsh and his teacher Ishaq Khatlani are reported to have revolted against the Timurid ruler Shah Rukh in 1413, and were consequently imprisoned, the life of Nurbakhsh being spared but Khatlani being put to death on account of his popularity at large.

The Nurbakhshi order of dervishes was an offshoot from the Kubravi order. Nurbakhsh is strongly associated with Shi'i beliefs, but his pupil Shamsuddin Muhammad al-Lahiji (d.1515) took an independent tangent from the Nurbakhshi order and was active in Shiraz.

50. Cf. Shea and Troyer trans., Vol. 1, p. 133. On the non-Zoroastrian Kaivanis cf. Modi, *art. cit.*, pp. 49 ff.
51. M. Boyce, *op. cit.*, p. 158.
52. Cf. my remarks on the ecological theories of cultural materialist anthropology in my *Psychology in Science* (Cambridge: Anthropographia Publications, 1983), pp. 161–2.
53. Cf. Shea and Troyer trans., Vol. 1, pp. 137–8.
54. As Rieu (*op. cit.*) early observed, Mobad Shah resided in Surat, Hyderabad, and lastly Srikakul "the capital of Kalingah, on the Coromandel coast A.H. 1061–63."
55. S.H. Nasr, *An Introduction to Islamic Cosmological Doctrines* (1978), p. 10, whose translation of *hakim* as "theosopher" does not meet with the agreement of other scholars.
56. Cf. Shea and Troyer trans., Vol. 3, p. 205.
57. A.S. Bazmee Ansari, "Al-Damad" in *The Encyclopaedia of Islam* (new edn) Vol. 2 (1965), pp. 103–4. See also H. Corbin, *En Islam Iranien,* Vol. 4 (1972) pp. 9–53.
58. Nasr, "The School of Ispahan," pp. 914 ff. The symbology of the Yemen is traceable to much earlier references in the Jabirian corpus. See Nasr, *Islamic Cosmological Doctrines,* p. 38 n. 60.
59. Cf. Shea and Troyer trans., Vol. 3, p. 204.
60. M. Bayat, *Mysticism and Dissent: Socioreligious Thought in Qajar Iran* (New York: Syracuse University Press, 1982), pp. 28 ff. In an above average work of historical endeavour, Bayat arguably renders the thesis less historical by including a statement concerning the "theosophers" that "far from being scientists, they were merely theologians defending preconceived positions." While this judgment may well be true of certain figures of the era in question, if it is extended to Mulla Sadra, Damad, Findiriski, and even the more theological polymath Amili, then arguably a serious error is likely to be committed. Cf. S.H. Nasr, *Sadr al-Din Shirazi and his Transcendent Theosophy* (1978), pp. 31 ff. on the life of Sadra, from which it emerges that the last period of his life as a teacher at Shiraz is of uncertain length, though it may have lasted for as long as thirty years or so. For Corbin's version of Sadra, cf. *En Islam Iranien,* Vol. 4 (Paris: Gallimard, 1972), pp. 54–122, which starts off with a well-annotated biographical review but then accelerates into more Corbinesque themes. See also J.W. Morris, trans. and with

introduction, *The Wisdom of the Throne: An Introduction to the Philosophy of Mulla Sadra* (Princeton, N.J.: Princeton University Press, 1981).

61. See my *Psychology in Science* (1983), pp. 87 ff. on Kepler, pp. 98 ff. on Newton.

62. S.H. Nasr, "Sadr al-Din Shirazi (Mulla Sadra)" (932–961) in M.M. Sharif, ed., *A Hist. of Muslim Philos. Vol. 2* (1966), p. 934.

63. Said Amir Arjomand, "Religious Extremism (*Ghuluww*), Sufism and Sunnism in Safavid Iran: 1501–1722," *Jnl of Asian History* (Wiesbaden 1981), 15:1–35, pp. 27–8.

64. See *ibid.*, pp. 6–7 and n. 25.

65. Arjomand unhesitatingly designates Findiriski as a sufi, and observes that he travelled to India, and became a recluse for seven years (*ibid.*, p. 23).

66. On Kabir and his literary legacy, see C. Vaudeville, *Kabir Vol. 1* (Oxford: Clarendon Press, 1974). Dara Shikoh described Baba Lal as a shaven-headed monk and a follower of Kabir, though Rizvi favours a description as a well-informed Vaishnavite mendicant. Though Qanungo formerly assumed that Shikoh and Baba Lal conversed in Urdu, it appears that the talks were actually in the Hindi dialect then common amongst sadhus in North India. Rizvi suggests that Shikoh may have learnt this dialect from sufi poetry composed in Hindi. See Rizvi, *A History of Sufism in India Vol. 2* (New Delhi: Munshiram Manoharlal, 1983), pp. 414 ff. It is apparent that Baba Lal mentioned both *fana* and *baqa*, and hence these oft-simplified sufi terms had been appropriated by Hindu ascetics.

67. M. Mahfuz-Ul-Haq, trans., *Majma'-ul-Bahrain or the Mingling of the Two Oceans by Prince Mhd Dara Shikuh* (Calcutta: Asiatic Society of Bengal, *Bibliotheca Indica,* 1929), translator's intro.

68. M. Prasad, "The Unpublished Translation of the Upanishads by Prince Dara Shikoh" (622–638) in *Dr. Modi Memorial Volume* (Bombay: K.J. Dubash, 1930) pp. 626–7.

69. S.A.A. Rizvi, *Muslim Revivalist Movements in Northern India in the Sixteenth and Seventeenth Centuries* (Agra: Agra University, 1965), pp. 354 ff.; *id.*, "The Muslim Ruling Dynasties" (245–65) in A.L. Basham, ed., *A Cultural Hist. of India,* pp. 262–4. On Dara Shikoh, see also Rizvi, *A Hist. of Sufism in India Vol. 2* (1983), pp. 122 ff, 413 ff. Still a major work of

reference is B.J. Hasrat, *Dara Shikuh: His Life and Works* (Visvabharati, Shantiniketan, 1953; repr. New Delhi, 1982).

70. S.D. Sekhri, "Prince Dara Shikuh and his Persian Translation of the Upanishads," *Indo-Iranica* (Calcutta 1959) 12(3): 1–9, p. 1.

71. According to Rizvi, it seems that Aurangzeb obtained initiation into the Naqshbandi order in 1666, through the intervention of Shaikh Muhammad Masum (*A Hist. of Sufism in India Vol. 2,* p. 485). This refers to the bigoted Naqshbandi sect known as the Mujaddidiyya.

72. Cf. Rizvi, *A Hist. of Sufism in India Vol. 2,* pp. 144–5. Badakshi was Shikoh's first *murshid,* and maintained a permanent connection with the royal family. Shikoh's second *murshid* Shaikh Bari had died in 1652. The letters of the prince to the *pir* Shah Muhammad Dilruba are undated. Shikoh referred to Sarmad as "my *pir* and *murshid.*" The verses in Shikoh's *Diwan* are modelled upon the poems of Jami and Mahmud Shabistari.

73. Rizvi, *op. cit.,* p. 414, citing K.R. Qanungo, *Dara Shukoh* (Calcutta 1935), pp. 34–49. It was immediately after the Qandahar campaign that the prince encountered Baba Lal, who probably strongly disapproved of such practices.

74. Rizvi, *op. cit.,* p. 424, observing that a large number of manuscript copies of Shikoh's translation of the Upanishads are available in libraries and private collections of both Hindus and Muslims in India.

75. On the subject of Sarmad, see B.A. Hashmi, "Sarmad, his life and quatrains," *Islamic Culture* (Hyderabad, Deccan, 1933) 7: 663–72, and *Islamic Culture* (1934) 8: 92–104, who deduces that Sarmad's emigrant ancestors appear to have been European Jews who moved to Armenia; W.J. Fischel, "Jews and Judaism at the Court of the Moghul Emperors in Medieval India," *Islamic Culture* (1951) 25: 105–132, pp. 119 ff, urging that Sarmad's Jewish origin played a decisive part in the reasons for his execution; Rizvi, *Muslim Revivalist Movements . . . .* (1965), pp. 343–4, 366 ff; *id., A Hist. of Sufism in India Vol. 2,* pp. 475 ff, who classifies Sarmad as a *majzub,* a sufi term which could yet do with some tighter appraisals as to its precise meaning.

76. Maulavi Abdul Wali, "A Sketch of the Life of Sarmad," *Jnl of the Asiatic Society of Bengal* (Calcutta 1924) 20: 111–122, p. 115.

77. Hashmi, 1934 *art. cit.,* p. 93. Maulavi Abdul Wali had earlier

observed that quatrains of other authors had been mixed with those of Sarmad in the typical process affecting collections of Persian poems (1924 *art. cit.,* p. 120). Earlier still, the Maulavi had observed that Sarmad's poems consist mostly of quatrains, of which no complete collection had been published, though a few of these *rubaiyat* had been lithographed at Bombay and Delhi; Rieu had noted that more than 400 *rubaiyat* attributed to Sarmad were preserved in ms. in the British Museum (Maulavi Abdul Wali, "Sarmad: His Life and Execution," *Indian Antiquary,* Bombay 1910, 34: 119–126, p. 121). Fischel said that more than 300 quatrains are ascribed to Sarmad in various manuscripts, and notes that he had seen a printed copy of Sarmad's *Rubaiyat,* ed. by Nawab Kishor of Lucknow, in a Paris library (Fischel, *art. cit.,* p. 121). J. Marek observed that a few of Sarmad's quatrains are preserved in the *Dabistan,* and that his quatrains as a whole testify to his endeavour to create a rapprochement between Islam and Hinduism. Marek did not neglect to stress that Sarmad's early studies in Iran particularly included natural science. See J. Marek, "Persian Literature in India" (713–734) in J. Rypka *et al, A History of Iranian Literature* (Dordrecht: Reidel, 1968), pp. 728–9.

78. Rizvi, *Muslim Revivalist Movements,* pp. 370 ff; Mujeeb, *The Indian Muslims,* p. 311, citing the *Muntakhab al-Lubab* of Khafi Khan; Rizvi, *A Hist. of Sufism in India Vol. 2,* pp. 170–2.

79. Rizvi, *Muslim Revivalist Movements,* pp. 334 ff; Mujeeb, *The Indian Muslims,* pp. 309–10.

80. A. Schimmel, *Islam in the Indian Subcontinent* (1980), p. 101.

81. Rizvi, *op. cit.,* p. 427.

82. E.g., Trimingham's glossary alternative of "existential monism" is arguably misleading, though his "unicity of Being" is much nearer the mark (*The Sufi Orders in Islam,* p. 313).

83. Quoted in, e.g., *Selections from the Rubaiyat and Odes of Hafiz,* by a member of the Persia Society of London (London: John M. Watkins, 1920), p. 14.

84. Another commentator to express an appreciation of the *Dabistan* was the Muslim scholar Maulavi Abdul Wali, who opined that the author was "of uncommon power of observation and research," and not neglecting to add that C. Rieu had considered this author a Zoroastrian in his *Cat. of the Persian*

Manuscripts in the British Museum. See M.A. Wali, 1924 *art. cit.*, p. 11. The Jewish scholar Fischel referred to the *Dabistan* as "one of the most outstanding works which has ever been produced in the Persian language on comparative religion." (W.J. Fischel, *art. cit.*, p. 122). In his introduction to the one-volume American edition of the Shea and Troyer trans. of the *Dabistan* (New York, 1901), A.V. Williams Jackson fairly commented on it as "a work by an Oriental and written for Orientals, but we of the West may equally profit by its contents."

85. Subsequently printed in a single volume edition in 1809 at Calcutta, of which two copies reside in C.U.L., one of them from the library of another Sanskritist, Prof. Edward Byles Cowell.

86. Cf. Modi, 1932 *art. cit.*, pp. 82–3, and see note 5 *supra*. Modi gives the information that the treatise in question was republished in 1842 with some explanatory additions by Fardunji Marzban, the Kaivani-type sadhu. It was also translated into Arabic by Shaikh Abu Barakat of Baghdad.

87. H. Beveridge, trans., *The Akbarnama of Abu'l Fazl Vol. 3* (Calcutta: Asiatic Society of Bengal, *Bibliotheca Indica,* 1910), p. 158.

88. *Ibid.,* pp. 160 ff.

89. A recent attempt to set Zarathushtra in a more accurate chronological and geographical perspective is G. Gnoli, *Zoroaster's Time and Homeland* (Naples: Istituto Universitario Orientale, 1980), enlarging upon his Sistan hypothesis. Cf. M. Boyce, Chapter Eleven in *The Cambridge History of Judaism Vol. 1* (Cambridge University Press, 1984), holding to *c.* 1500–1300 as the date of Zarathushtra. Cf. my *Minds and Sociocultures* (forthcoming), Part Two.

APPENDIX 1: THE DESATIR

It is an interesting possibility that not a few modern manifestations of Western occultism owe their origin, however indirectly, to a misunderstood and now almost completely ignored treatise of the Kaivani tradition. This treatise was procured from Iran, though it may well have been penned or edited in India.

The *Desatir* was particularly appealing to nineteenth century Theosophists like Olcott owing to its alignment with Hindu–Buddhistic lore. But a close inspection of the treatise, even in the English translation, reveals that the similarity with Theosophical beliefs is superficial in many respects.

The *Desatir* has been viewed askance by literalist scholars of Zoroastrianism, and detested by orthodox Parsi religionists. A less biased appraisal came from Ibrahim Pur-Davud, the Iranian scholar who was admirably sympathetic to Zoroastrian history, and who understandably stressed that the *Desatir* is not an original Pahlavi document, though he does not appear to have grasped the significance of the Kaivani phenomenon.

That an individual, or individuals, of some grouping of the Kaivani–ishraqi stream should have penned a work stating the pre-Islamic origins of their tradition should not seem surprising; even if poorly rendered from some more dexterous mind or hand, the basic contentions are arresting and in keeping with the expansive outlook of a Maqtul, not forgetting some of the Zurvanites and others of ancient Iran. The *Desatir* is perhaps an inferior document from the literary point of view compared to other ishraqi-type treatises, but it makes its point. The *Desatir* was certainly available from 1818 to an interested cross-cultural audience, and one suspects that a few of its themes may have been appropriated without acknowledgment even via third-hand garbled report.

It is not known whether the *Desatir* had any specific personal connection with Azar Kaivan, who lived out his mature years in the tolerant climate of Akbarian India, ostensibly in a rather solitary maneouvre, and who for all anybody knows, may have been the leading "master" of his time as extant Kaivani works affirm. The full title accorded him was *Qutub-i azam, Ghaus-i alam wa Imam-i zaman* (Supreme Pole, Helper of the world, Imam of the time). Suffice it to say that there is no mention of "masters" in the Western Theosophical sense in the *Desatir*; the theme is instead that of a succession of prophets who periodically emerge to revive a teaching that is continually obscured by man.

Turning to a consideration of the manuscript of the *Desatir* published by Dastur Mulla Firuz, the version of the "Fifth Sasan" gives a translation of, and commentary on, the original "Sacred Writings." The language of the latter was termed *asmani* ("celestial language"), and an interested panel of European scholars pronounced some cold judgments on its authenticity. In the *Asiatic Journal* of 1820, the British scholar Norris referred to the language of the *Desatir* text as an invented jargon. Sylvestre de Sacy also decided against the antiquity of the work, and William Von Schlegel described the *asmani* as a "refined forgery." A century later Modi cited a more recent paper prepared by the Parsi priest and scholar Sheriarji Dadabhai Bharucha for an International Congress of Orientalists at Geneva, which appropriately observed that the syntax of the *Desatir* betrayed its recent origin, and described its language as "a conventional jargon composed of later Pahlavi, Persian and Hindi dialects." Modi added that he did not think that the *asmani* language should be called an intentional forgery, since "some mystic writers aim at a kind of secrecy in the expression of their doctrines," i.e., the author had employed what he considered to be a suitably esoteric vehicle of expression constructed from the dialects of the different countries from which his teachings derived. Modi also expressed his view that the unknown author of the *Desatir* was a Parsi *mobad* (J.J. Modi, *Jnl of the K.R. Cama Oriental Institute,* 1932, 20: 18–20, 16).

Ethe described the *asmani* language of the *Desatir* as "a kind of fictitious language," which he considered to have afforded a "secret medium of communication" among the members of a theosophical sect (H. Ethe, *Catalogue of*

Persian Manuscripts in the Library of the India Office Vol. 1, Oxford 1903, cols 1523–4).

Turning to a consideration of the English aspect of the 1818 publication in Bombay by Dastur Mulla Firuz, the latter remarks in his editorial preface that the *Desatir* was known to have existed during the reign of Shah Jahan (since it is mentioned in the *Dabistan*), but had eluded the search of the curious in later times. The attention of the European world was first directed to it by Sir William Jones, who commented on the chapter in the *Dabistan* which outlines the "religion of Hushang," which is indicated to have been much older than that of Zarathushtra. This Hushangian tradition had continued to be secretly professed by many learned Iranians. Several of these latter moved to India under the pressures of persecution, and there they compiled a number of books – now extremely scarce observed Jones – which the author of the *Dabistan* had studied, and with whose compilers (or with some of them) he had contracted a close friendship (Mulla Firuz, pp. I–II).

Hushang is one of the prophets included in the *Desatir,* though not the first in the series, an honour accorded to Mahabad, with whom was associated a rather complex dynastic legend. The Iranian emigrants mentioned in the *Dabistan* formed the core of the Kaivani groups in Mughal India.

Mulla Firuz went on to observe that the author of the *Dabistan* frequently mentions the *Desatir,* and adopted it as his guiding source of reference in the account of the "religious dynasties of Mahabad and his successors," of whom Zarathushtra was one. During the reign of the Mughal emperor Shah Jahan, the reputation of the *Desatir* must have been high (even amongst Muslims), since Hakim ibn Khalif ut-Tabrizi Muhammad Husain often quoted its commentary as his authority for words in the old Persian in his dictionary of the Persian language. Yet though the *Desatir* had frequently been referred to by Persian writers, it was evidently regarded as the sacred book of a particular sect, and appears to have been accordingly guarded via an uncommunicative method that has particularly hallmarked

Eastern sects. It is therefore logical to expect that the contents would have been known in more depth to the members of the sect. It is accordingly quoted, adds Firuz, by Farzaneh Behram ibn Farhad, author of the *Sharistan-i chahar chaman*. Mulla Firuz describes this Iranian as a man who "though outwardly a Musselman, was really a Parsi, or rather a disciple of Azer Keiwan." Kaivan is in turn described by Firuz as "a philosophical ascetic who founded a new sect on the foundation of the ancient Parsi tenets" (Mulla Firuz, pp. VI–VII). If by "Parsi," one substituted the expression = an Irani version of ishraqi teachings which in turn borrowed from the Irani Zoroastrian tradition, then one might be nearer the ancient truth.

The editor of the *Desatir* explains how the manuscript came to be in his possession. It was the only manuscript of the treatise known to exist, and had been purchased at Isfahan by his father Mulla Kaus about forty-five years earlier. A bookseller had come to know that Kaus was a Parsi, and had accordingly taken the manuscript to him in the hope of making a sale, being prompted by the words written on the cover which declared it as *Kitab-i Gabri* (Book of the unbeliever) in the typical idiom of stigma. Mulla Kaus had accordingly invested in it, particularly since he had been sent by the Parsis of India to travel in Iran for the purpose of ascertaining details about the Zoroastrian remnant there.

Though Mulla Firuz appears to have been a conscientious linguist for his time, he dwells with brevity on the text of the *Desatir*. He evidently regarded the text as a very ancient document, and was subsequently criticized for this, and also for stating that the text was in a different language from the Zand, the Pahlavi, *and* Dari. But he was arguably correct in deeming the appended Pahlavi-style commentary of the Fifth Sasan as displaying "a very subtle and refined metaphysics." Neither the commentary nor the text are at all ritual in character.

A pertinent item in the commentary is the stipulation that when a Yazdani (=Hushangian) is asked "What is your religion?" the answer should be the religion acceptable to Yazdan. But in circumstances involving risk, "the concealment and hiding of his faith is necessary" (Firuz–Erskine trans., p. 187).

In the midst of a long metaphysical commentary on the First Sasan, an ishraqi-based rationale is discernible in the explanation that writings of the Prophet Hushang allow the young student to know the Absolute by proofs deduced from reason; subsequently the student should devote himself to a programme of seclusion, meditation, and abstinence in order to gain perception of Yazdan and "those who are near to the Most Just (*Dadar*)" (ibid, p. 163).

It is relevant in this connection that the Zoroastrian ishraqis of Akbar's time maintained the contemplative and dialectical forms of training of the mind, in accordance with earlier precedents in the Iranian ishraqi tradition. The dialectical form was a continuation of the Peripatetic slant acquired from Greek models. The subject becomes complex for convenient summary because the dialectical form fits differing ratios, and some hold that advanced forms of it are superior to some contemplative modes. The average mentation involved in "deductive proofs" is however considered to be appreciably inferior to contemplation of any depth.

An interesting variant on this theme is included in the commentary on the section of the *Desatir* attributed to Zarathushtra. Some idea of how the aptitudes of "illumination" and "reason" were respectively viewed is afforded by the description of the former as having the power of leaving the body at will, of treating the body as a virtual garment – while the latter aptitude is conceived as discovering the real nature of things as they actually exist by means of reason *and* meditation (*ibid.*, p. 24). It is evident that the dialectic was more sophisticated than might at first seem. The treatise imparts a further twist to this subject by supplying the alleged context of ancient Iranians being superior to Greeks in "illumination," and antedating the Greeks in possessing "reason." Aristotle is here seen as the first Greek rationalist.

The section attributed to Zarathushtra states that his speech is of two kinds: the enigmatic and the unenigmatic. Yet there is a rationale supplied for the difference here. The prophet Jamshed is quoted as saying that mankind comprehend according to their knowledge, while the prophet speaks according to his own level of wisdom. But this also obligates the prophet to speak in accordance with the ordinary knowledge so that he might be understood by those lacking in wisdom (cf. *ibid.,* p. 99).

The *Desatir* does not express a highly flattering estimation of those who are not true seekers after truth, and affirms that it is impossible to "ascend the spheres and reach the stars and angels" unless the negative tendencies in the individual disposition are removed. Those who do not sufficiently discipline themselves do not achieve an ascendancy of the soul over the imagination, and therefore they "fashion what they observe according to the creations of their imagination." Their knowledge is thus equivalent to fancy (*ibid.,* p. 25). The metaphorical context fits the ishraqi tradition of angelology, a complex subject of symbolism, but here with the typical Kaivani–Mahabadian alignment of error with failure to observe *ahimsa* (non-violence), doubtless a jab at Islamic persecution.

"The human soul is independent, indivisible, without beginning or end" is an aphorism attributed to the First Sasan, and the commentary adds: "To one who attends to the understanding, the clearest of all things is his own existence and reality." There is the additional affirmation that the soul is a substance, and not an accident, since with the exception of Yazdan, whatever possesses being is either substance or accident (*ibid.,* pp. 173–4). Here one might well recognize a clarified precedent to the *cogito ergo sum* of Descartes, one that was furthermore cosmopolitan in its extensions, and with much more ancient connections not dependent upon modern transitions and fiascos which incorporated a mechanistic scheme that had no place for the souls of animals.

In the latter respect, the Mahabadian section (attributed to the prophet Mahabad) presents a distinctive disquisition on *ahimsa* which threatens retribution for the killing of harmless animals, but which permits the slaying of predatory and carnivorous animals. Predatory animals are depicted as the incarnations of grandees who have shed blood, while the harmless beasts of burden are simultaneously viewed as former men who imposed burdens upon others unjustly. An adroit castigation of Muslim oppressors? More extreme-sounding statements are that "foolish evildoers" become confined to the form of vegetables, and that those who cultivate harmful knowledge and work evil become confined to the form of minerals (*ibid.*, p. 15). It is evident, however, that there is a good deal of symbolism in the *Desatir,* conceivably confused by redactions and translations, though the exhortatory tone is frequently unenigmatic.

An example of explanation of metaphor is found in the Zarathushtra chapter where a lengthy dialogue between animals and men in the text is described by the commentary as a fable whose object is to recommend self-control and self-knowledge, since man has the ascendancy over other animals *only* by speech, ingenuity, knowledge, and appropriate conduct.

The author, or authors, would no doubt have agreed that the ascendancy of rather a lot of men in the modern day is only very marginally in advance of that of quadrupeds, and in not a few instances might even be said to resemble cauliflower status by comparison.

The Mahabadian exposition includes a brief reference to "grand cycles" of time, each of which resembles the preceding one by way of a recurrence – but *not* in exactly the same forms or events (*ibid.*, p. 21). Though brief, there is a resemblance to Zurvanite concepts here, concepts which date back at least to the Achaemenid era of Iran, and are therefore as old by extant standards as the more well-known *yugas* of Indian philosophy. Some scholars believe that the teachings about *zurvan* (time) were ultimately Babylonian, and if true, then the probable archaic nature of these concepts is pronounced.

The section of the *Desatir* dealing with tangible history predictably sides with the Sassanian *mobads* against Mazdak's "common property and women," (even modern scholarship finds it difficult to ascertain exactly what happened in this dissident religious movement), but is unsympathetic also to the earlier third century reformer Mani. The commentary observes Mani's asceticism, but accuses him of giving permission to slay harmless animals, which seems slender grounds for considering him a false prophet (*ibid.*, pp. 188 ff.). However, it had long been customary in both Islamic and Zoroastrian annals to denigrate Mani, and the *Desatir* is actually very mild on this subject by comparison with other sources, including some modern scholastic ones.

There is very much less of a Zoroastrian bias in the reference to the Prophet Muhammad, who though not listed as one of the Mahabadian series, is favourably referred to in the text as "an eloquent man and his words involved." Whatever the case for an enigmatic Semite here, his followers are unambiguously described as overthrowing the heedless Persians, but subsequently becoming divided by conflicts among themselves. The commentary adds that the defeated Zoroastrians adopted the foreign religion and created more sects which offset the victory of the invaders (*ibid.,* pp. 194–5). While the text evidently views the Arab invasion as a karmic retribution for the imperial Sassanians, the commentary can be interpreted as harbouring Shia sympathies or affinities.

The *Desatir* is not an easy book to read for the modern Westerner even in translation, but it is definitely distinctive by comparison with many religio-mystical and philosophical classics of the European Renaissance and post-Renaissance eras.

APPENDIX 2: THE BRITISH EMPIRE AND THE SIPASI PHILOSOPHERS

A revealing article penned by the historian William Erskine records this British scholar's estimation of the *Desatir* and the *Dabistan.* Best known for his researches into imperial Mughal history, he was one of the first Europeans to see the *Desatir,* being in contact with Mulla Firuz in Bombay. Erskine's article is dated 1818, and was written just prior to publication of the *Desatir.* He does not state that he had translated the latter work, but does say that he had recently had access to it. He reports that Governor Duncan of Bombay had undertaken a translation of it, which that official had persevered with for several years.

Erskine's communication appeared in the *Transactions of the Literary Society of Bombay* (London, 1820) Vol. 2: 342–76. It was entitled "On the Authenticity of the *Desatir,* with remarks on the account of the Mahabadi Religion contained in the *Dabistan.*" It is written in a critical vein, and in some respects is typical of general Empire attitudes to the native religions and philosophies. Erskine refers to the Kaivanis as the Sipasis, a legitimate alternative description, since the designation of Sipasi is applied to them by the author of the *Dabistan.* The term *sipasi* means "adorer," in the sense of a worshipper of the "sun," a reference to the elaborate system of symbolic associations to be found in Kaivani treatises. The term was not clarified by Erskine, and has remained an effective mystery in the general neglect and distortion of the subject under discussion (my choice of the new term Kaivani is in conscious contradiction of former misunderstandings).

Erskine was in large part reacting to the very literal views expressed by his predecessor Sir William Jones, who had assumed that the *Dabistan* references to early Iranian "dynasties" were historical. Erskine was quite correct in rebutting this assumption of Jones, but went to the other extreme in deciding that there was little or no value in Sipasi works owing to their allegorical portrayals.

Erskine was also in reaction to the views of Mulla Firuz,

who had assumed that the *Desatir* was an ancient pre-Islamic treatise. Again, the British scholar was accurate enough in concluding a much more recent date for this work, but he allowed other biases to distort his interpretation, biases that were possibly much more confusing than those of his learned associate.

After demolishing the Jonesian literalism, Erskine goes on to review the contents of the *Desatir,* which he was using as proof that Jones was hopelessly wrong. As perhaps with many other scholarly dramas of this type, deeper aspects of the contested data passed without due comment. To Erskine, it was merely a scornful reflection upon allegory that "the religion of Mahabad is presented to us as a secret religion which has not been openly professed for many thousand years." Erskine had located what he took to be the dead-end origin of the *Dabistan* statements on Iranian "history": a sectarian treatise of simulated Pahlavi auspices which could not possibly contain the truths for which historians vied, the stuff of history – of monarchies, governments, empires, wars, and all the other similarly important ingredients which comprised civilization as it was known to the Reason of Europe.

Some readers may well conclude that *Desatir* data, even in Erskine's contraction, is more interesting than skeletons of historical argument. For instance, Erskine faithfully reports the teaching that the world is subject to periodical destruction at the end of grand cycles of time that comprise "a period of many millions of years." In each of these grand cycles, as in the system of Plato adds our commentator, the planets commence their revolutions from the same points, and a new series of events ensues in the world, "exactly similar to what has already occurred in an infinite series of preceding cycles" (p. 351). But Erskine gives the wrong sense here, since the *Desatir* states that the recurrences are not exact. Such scholarly slips of the pen may conceal vast dimensions of cosmic meaning, particularly when one realizes that the theme is that of the precession of the equinoxes, i.e. the "Great Year," celebrated in ancient lore with varying degrees of skill and complexity.

In his routine review, Erskine states that the words

attributed to the prophets of the *Desatir* consist in large part of "liturgical addresses to the Supreme Being" (p. 354). But the word liturgical is misleading here, since the unorthodoxy of the treatise is beyond question. Facts are not always reliably reported even by ardent factualists. The Supreme Being (Mezdam) specified in the chapter on Mahabad was reminiscent to Erskine of the Vedanta philosophy, though it is perhaps more accurately of a Zurvanite character. This Absolute is described in the *Desatir* as without beginning, without form, infinite, incomprehensible, creating – or causing to be created – a series of ministering "angels" who are assigned the work of creation and the direction of world events. The planetary associations are pronounced in this system, underlined in Erskine's observation that whereas the Supreme Being is addressed directly in the first four chapters (each synonymous with a prophet), in later chapters each prophet invokes the "intelligence" of a planet. This was mere astrological superstition to our Empire factualist, who missed the significance of the Sipasi emphasis that "the souls of the blest, which have shaken off impediments of the body, rise to the rank of angels (=planets), to ecstasy which the tongue cannot express, nor the ear hear, nor the human eye perceive" (p. 356). Instead, Erskine contented himself with finding a "sufi character" in the Sipasi ascetic injunctions, as if the label was sufficient to explain the subject. Self-denial, solitary meditation, and abstinence from meat and drink were not favoured attributes of Empire personnel, and conceivably the real reason why the Sipasis were not more historically esteemed.

Though the implications of solar "intelligence" were lost upon Erskine, he did conclude that "the planetary religion of the *Desatir* seems in part borrowed from the old Persian system, but in a far greater number of particulars from the ancient Chaldean" (p. 372). This reference to Chaldean antecedents is more historically to be specified as Sabean, a Near Eastern sequel to more archaic eras that was partially preserved in the writings of Arabic-speaking commentators. The Sabeans of Harran were by no means clear to Erskine, who was relying for his information upon Edward Pococke's version of Shahrastani in his *Specimen Historiae Arabum* (Oxford 1806), and the even less adequate *De Vetere Religione Persarum* (1700) of the Oxford orientalist Thomas Hyde. These substitutes of historical accident were no effective remedy for the complete absence of *ishraqi* particulars in Erskine's analysis. *Ishraqi* philosophy appears to have been entirely unknown to Erskine, who treated Sipasi works with a proportionate lack of perspective. The *ishraqi* tradition of Sohravardi Maqtul had assimilated aspects of the Sabean lore, but in general this lore has not been adequately evaluated. (On this subject, see my *Sufis, Batinis, Scientists and Philosophers of the early Islamic era,* chapter seven).

Since he was entirely ignorant of the historical basis of the Sipasi events, it is less surprising that Erskine commented non-perceptively on the story of the Greek (Yunani) sage and that concerning Alexander the Great in the chapter attributed to Zarathushtra (Zartusht). "This is evidently an attempt to derive the philosophy of the Greeks from Persia" (p. 358). In fact, it is rather something quite different, possessing clear features of *ishraqi* symbolism which incorporates a play upon the associations of "east" and "west," where the sun rises and sets. (On these and other stories in the *Desatir,* see my *The Resurrection of Philosophy,* chapter nine).

With regard to derivations, Erskine himself was remarkably bold in his theory of Persian borrowings from Europe. He observed that the chapter in the *Desatir* attributed to the "First Sasan" possesses a sophisticated metaphysical commentary setting forward proofs of the existence and attributes of the Absolute, "with elucidations of the nature of spirit and the senses." But we are told that "it may safely be affirmed that no such train of reasoning is to be found in any Persian work more than three hundred years old" (pp. 358–9). The opinion is subsequently expressed that "many of the acute metaphysical remarks" in the commentary as a whole were derived from the schoolmen of Latin Europe rather "than directly from the Oriental or Aristotelian philosophy." This was arguably an invention of sheer myth from an historicist. While the deadline for Persian expressions is feasible, the Arabic treatises of the ishraqi tradition belie such assumptions of historical vacuum on the part of factualists. Erskine might have been advised to study the intricacies of allegory rather than to construct an excised history equivalent to uninstructive make-believe. (Mobad Shah does not specify that the "Oriental" philosophy was equivalent to the ishraqi, but even if he had indulged in this tautology, the Sipasi orientation would have seemed double dutch to those biased in favour of a European version of Greek philosophy).

The panpsychism of the *Desatir* was briefly passed over by our commentator. It was neither a Christian nor a rationalist or empiric doctrine that everything possesses a soul, even minerals, with all the entities of nature capable of a continual and unlimited improvement towards an ultimate perfection. Erskine comments: "The system of the metemphsychosis pervades the whole; a remarkable circumstance, in which the *Desatir* differs from all other systems of Persian mythology, and agrees with those of India" (p. 355). Note how panpsychism is relegated to mythology, again a non-factual deduction as it happens, since earlier Iranian exponents of the medieval era had favoured the subject, not to mention the pre-Islamic Manichaeans. Unlike some other staid critics however, Erskine did not berate this subject, and even paused to comment that this viewpoint "naturally leads to a mild and humane treatment of the lower animals."

By comparison with various other statements, Erskine's analysis of the linguistic components of the *Desatir* was factually accurate. He observes that the text includes a great majority of words which belong to no known tongue, and displays a mixture of Persian and Indian words, while a few Arabic words also occur. Many of the words of Indian origin are of Sanskrit derivation, but others belong to the vernacular. He remarked that the accompanying Persian translation and commentary ascribed to the Sassanian son of the Fifth Sasan are "extremely curious," comprising many antiquated words, but showing no admixture whatever of "words of Arabic or Chaldaic origin." The latter omission is not surprising, but it is true enough that Arabic words are found in the early Persian of Tabari and Firdausi, hence leading to the valid conclusion that the Persian of the *Desatir* is too well formed a language to be as early as the ascription might suggest. Erskine clearly felt that here was proof of the pseudo-nature of the treatise, and tended as a consequence to treat the contents as an aberration. Later commentators were more liberal and perceptive in their view of the usage intended for the *Desatir*. The fascination with bizarre alphabets, including very cryptic varieties, is traceable to gnostic trends in the early Islamic era; the "esoteric" scripts were considered one means of counteracting orthodox religious dogmatism.

No such considerations of high-flown attributions in provenance apply to the *Dabistan,* which clearly states its date of authorship in the later Mughal era. But Erskine proceeded to give this treatise a more severe analytical judgment than he had expressed for the *Desatir* (see *ibid.,* pp. 364 ff). Of Mobad Shah, he writes: "His work has all the excellencies and defects that might be expected from the mode in which it was compiled. As the author was extremely tolerant, he did not consider a difference in rites or forms as of any moment." One can agree with the first sentence here, but the second is extremely questionable; Mobad Shah gives several indications of his "observer" stance, as distinct from that of a participant. The incongruities of differing religious attitudes are pointed out in a sophisticated manner unlikely to cause offence. Erskine mentions approvingly Mobad Shah's impartiality (which is too obvious even for critics to ignore), but adds "it is equally clear that he was credulous, and, without perhaps being the sectary of any one religion, had a mind strongly tinged with superstition." As proof of this assertion, the British critic cites the autobiographical reference to the cure of a fever by astrological recourse, merely through the action of a brahmin immersing the image of a planet in water and making an incantation. It may be added that Mobad Shah was here deferring to Hindu astrology. Apart from any complexities in language, Mobad Shah may well have believed in the power of astrology; so do many modern intelligent Westerners, and hence he is not for that reason to be zero-rated.

There exists the question as to whether he possessed the same understanding of materials as the Kaivani circles he had earlier known; it is not necessary to assume this as a matter of course, and any disparity would not alter the basic value of his contribution. One reason for the elaborate secrecy and symbolism in some circles was to ensure that only the inessentials of "sectarian lore" were freely available for distortion or superficial rendition. This did not necessarily mean an unwillingness to educate a majority; Mobad Shah's own attempt to educate a readership has often fallen upon resistant ground.

Erskine commenced his attack in earnest with the observation that the *Dabistan* gives an abstract of the *Desatir* doctrines, "but with a strong Sufi cast," padded out with quotes from sufi poets. The critic was trying to establish the absence of historical material in the "Sabean" section of the *Dabistan* chapter on Zoroastrian sects. This was in an effort to decisively refute the conclusions of Jones and Mulla Firuz. But Mulla Firuz was perhaps less of a literalist than either of his British peers. While Erskine's conditioned viewpoint inevitably regarded all talk of "astrology" as mere superstition, it is more questionable that he recognized allegory without giving it any credence as such. "The conquest and destruction of the demons, they (the Sipasis) hold to mean only the conquest of man over his passions." This accusation could have been made by any hidebound theologian. "In like manner the whole history of Ky Khusro (*sic*), and of Alexander the Great, is reduced to a moral and allegorical romance." He neglected to add that the Sipasis were here following a long-established tradition in Arabic and Persian annals, and that Kai Khusrau and Alexander (alias Iskandar) had been invested with ishraqi significances of much stronger import than moralism or romance. (This is the reason for the appearance of Iskandar as one of the "prophets" in the *Desatir,* an inclusion which has seemed so anomalous to those unfamiliar with background nuance).

Continuing with his critique of the *Dabistan*, Erskine remarks: "The accounts given of the wars and hunting-matches of the ancient Pishdadi kings, being inconsistent with the supposed injunction not to kill, are also allegorized more absurdly, but in a much less fanciful and amusing strain, than are the struggles of a good Christian, or the operations of the loom, in the puritanical volumes of Bunyan's *Holy War,* or *The Whole Art of Weaving Spiritualized.*" This British witticism can perhaps be taken less seriously than the attempt to eradicate the wars and hunts of which the Empire was so fond at that time.

The teachings and practices of the Sipasi philosophers, in Erskine's view, were "evidently taken partly from the Sufis of Persia, partly from the Yogis of India." This is perhaps true enough in a general sense, but lack of precision renders the definition largely meaningless. No clarifications are forthcoming, and Erskine instead presses his chief obsession to an extreme: "All the ascetic practices . . . are altogether Hindu, and can throw no light whatever on the ancient history of Persia." As a matter of fact, some of the ascetic practices were not specifically Hindu, being fairly common in Iran, and arguably have strong kinship with early Manichaean and related trends that until recently have passed unnoticed in textual remains (see Shepherd, *Ancient Cultures in Flux,* final part).

In a footnote, our commentator adds: "I consider the greatest part of the later Sufi doctrines as borrowed from India." This opinion can now be firmly rebutted. It may have made good sense to Erskinian historicism, but overwhelming evidence to the contrary renders it less tenable than allegory.

A very distinctive Sipasi contention reported in the *Dabistan* is that the Ka'aba of Mecca, the tomb of Muhammad at Medina, the temple of Jerusalem, the tomb of Ali at Najaf in Iraq, the neighbouring tomb of Imam Husayn at Kerbela, the Hindu temple of Dwaraka, "and in general every place of pilgrimage whatever," was originally a temple of planetary significance in the archaic Mahabadi system. The latitude of this claim is startling, particularly by comparison with the insular views of prehistory entertained by orthodox contemporaries of the Sipasi–Kaivanis. Erskine typically remarks: "This theory is supported by some false and ridiculous etymologies." But he did add that this perspective was "extremely favourable to the Sufi latitudinarians," since they could then go on pilgrimage to any of these places, though "with a jesuitical mental reservation keeping in mind their own theological tenets" (p. 366). This curious wording reflects Erskine's oddly weighted view of how the Sipasi philosophers thought, and pinpoints the scholarly confusion between orthodox theologians and less orthodox thinkers. The crux is that the term "sufi" was amorphous in Erskine's vocabulary.

"They allegorize the whole of their ancient history" was Erskine's contemptous accusation against the Sipasis. One wonders whether more tangible facts would have met with any comprehension. It is worth pointing out that knowledge of ancient temple cultures in the Near and Middle East was extremely diminutive in Erskine's day. Our commentator might have deemed it impossible that Sir John Marshall and others would a century later discover the remains of the obscure Indus civilization in India – which, strangely enough perhaps, was in the close proximity of Dwaraka on the west coast. Knowledge of ancient Mesopotamian sites was extremely slender in the early nineteenth century, and not greatly in advance of the orthodox Muslim *ulama* who declared that strange sculptures discovered in Assyria were the idols of the infidels and hence fit only for destruction, a mandate which was quite literally carried out. Not until much later in the century did the remains of Sumer and Akkad begin to be exhumed to any substantial extent, to the amazement of antiquaries who thought that nothing much had ever existed outside Greece, Rome, and Egypt. Mesopotamian sites like Barsippa and Uruk are still very imperfectly known, but their temple cults are likely to have been more factually reminiscent of the "Mahabadian" religion than the age of Reason exemplified by Erskine.

The "Sabean" section of the *Dabistan* emerges as a "labyrinth of confusion" in Erskine's opinion. But the ensuing section "seems to afford the clue" to the labyrinth, though one suspects that Erskine was the minotaur. The clue was effectively reasoned into obscurity. This ensuing section contains the biographies of the Sipasi–Kaivanis, "who appear to have attempted to introduce a system of

Sufism on a slight Parsi foundation." More sourly, "they pretended, without any evidence, to have existed in the most remote times," a reference to the detested Mahabadian pedigree. This commentarial animosity is carried over into the estimation of Azar Kaivan, who "pretended to have received much of his knowledge in dreams and visions, from the philosophers of Greece, India and Persia." There is no credit given to the liberality of view demonstrated by the maligned philosopher, though there is the grudging acknowledgment that "he attended little to exterior worship, a peculiarity of all Sufis" (Erskine does not declare himself a ritualist, whatever his own peculiarities may have been). However, to cap this portrayal of pretence, there is the deduction that : "his (Kaivan's) scholars (i.e. disciples), though some of them were certainly men of talent and learning, have in general far too much the air of conjurors and jugglers."

The extraordinary fact about this latter appraisal is its slight foundation of proof adduced. Though very much a historian looking for historical information, Erskine chose to ignore the solid data of the biographies and related references in the Sipasi section of the *Dabistan*. Instead, he gives an extremely biased review of this biographical supplement in only two pages (pp. 369–370), and focussed only upon the more figurative ingredients of this material. In order to make his case firm against Jones and Mulla Firuz, he was evidently determined not to relent in his characterization of Sipasi data as an irrelevant aberration. Fortunately, the extant text reveals the extent of the excision.

The accusation of jugglery is based entirely upon the reported deportment of Yazdan Sitai, who was a pupil of Mobad Sarosh and not Kaivan, and who was posterior in time to the entire Zoroastrian circle of the latter. Sitai is certainly described in a more "yogic" idiom, but even if it is construed that he resorted to optical deception in the display of wonders, it may be no more than proof of a literalist tendency to treat hyperbole as proof of conjuring on the part of an entire sect. What were good Christians and colonialists to make of natives with a reputation for the power of separating their self from the body, to leave the body at will, "rendering themselves invisible to the eyes of men"? The historical implications of the Sipasi episode were certainly invisible to the eyes of Erskine and those who agreed with him.

Mobad Shah may have embellished the factual record with flourishes typical of Persian works at that era, but the content of the section under discussion is not as Erskine represented it. Hagiography was standard fare in sufi compendiums, but the *Dabistan* did not employ it to prove the superiority of either Islam or Zoroastrianism. Nuances in hyperbole were lost upon Erskine, but an understanding of these is necessary in the evaluation of some Persian texts. Parastar is referred to contemptuously as standing upon his head from twilight to dawn; more surprisingly, Antun Bashuyah is dismissed as choosing "to show his philosophy by going about stark naked." Erskine might have made good company for the carping *ulama* at Aurangzeb's court when they sought to charge the naked Sarmad with heretical aberration. One cannot therefore expect that the more complex references to Farshidwerd and Khiridmend would be tolerably explicated, as indeed they were not; these were two Zoroastrian disciples of Kaivan who are treated obliquely by Mobad Shah, who appears to have encountered them during his childhood. Erskine concludes that the Sipasis were in the habit of quarrelling amongst themselves, but it may well be that talent and the jugglery of erudition have been underestimated by those less dexterous in literary legerdemain. A Sarmadic pun may arouse the *shaitan* in the pedant.

"Is it by the writings of such dupes and knaves that we are to reform the history of ancient ages?" asked Erskine, in reference to the Sipasi philosophers. One can quite confidently answer: Not if the interpreters are literalist dupes and colonialist knaves seeking to reform the history of alien traditions in consonance with preconceived ideas of historical priorities.

A more reasonable perspective was the conclusion of the same writer that the *Desatir* originated in the Sipasi school, and that the *Dabistan* author was a Sipasi. Yet the mode of interpretation accompanying these deductions is a sad reflection upon an early phase of literalist historicism.

A note was appended to Erskine's communication which contributed the very feasible suggestion that it was not Muhsin Fani who authored the *Dabistan*. Here Erskine was again opposing a Jonesian supposition, but in this instance his insistence has withstood the test of time. The only account of Muhsin Fani that he could discover was that contained in a (then) recent work by one Lakshmi Narayan, an inhabitant of Hyderabad, who did not mention the *Dabistan*. Erskine converged with Mulla Firuz on the subject of the poetical name Mobad Shah, facilitated by a marginal note to the manuscript of the *Dabistan* owned by Mulla Firuz (see above, Part Two, note 43). But both Erskine and Mulla Firuz seem to have assumed that Mobad Shah was a Muslim, a view which did not alter until later in the century. It is still very difficult to be definitive as to the author's religious background, and I will not be dogmatic on this point. If he was born a Muslim, then he was reared in the close proximity of Zoroastrians and Hindus, and thought very much in a liberal Sipasi manner. Further, even if a Muslim background is considered a possibility, it is most unlikely that it is the case history of Muhsin Fani that is autobiographically referred to in the *Dabistan,* though Fani's poetry is quoted.

Erskine refers to the coincidence of his own theory of authorship with that of "the learned Vans Kennedy," whose relevant article appeared in the same volume of the *Bombay Transactions*. Captain Vans Kennedy had penned his "Notice Respecting the Religion Introduced into India by the Emperor Akbar" (242–270), an early probe into the *din-i-ilahi* which drew upon the *Dabistan,* which includes a section eulogistic of Akbar. Wrote the Captain: "That it was not Muhsin Fani, as supposed by Sir William Jones, is evident from every account which has been given of his life either by biographers or historians" (p. 243). Muhsin Fani is reported to have been made a chief judge at Allahabad by Shah Jahan after being in attendance at the Delhi court, and Vans Kennedy deemed this proof that the subject was an orthodox Muslim, an identity disqualifying him for authorship of the *Dabistan,* since "no true believer would ever have ventured to compose such a work as the *Dabistan.*" But this reflects the ideas of Islamic orthodoxy entertained by the British at that time (though it is to be conceded that those given such positions were prepared to accept conservative standards). Lakshmi Narayan affords evidence that Muhsin Fani was of sufi affiliation prior to his official appointment, and that while he held office at Allahabad, he became a disciple of Shaikh Muhibbullah, the heretical Chishti teacher. His orthodoxy was very sublimated by wujudi inclinations therefore. However, parallel dates that can be extrapolated indicate that Mobad Shah was otherwise occupied, and that it is different sufi entities we are discussing here.

The deduction of Vans Kennedy that the *Dabistan* author could not have been performing the duties of the *sadarut* at Allahabad is convincing enough without recourse to standard notions of orthodoxy. There are over fifty autobiographical dates given in the *Dabistan,* and from the early 1630's until 1649, Mobad Shah was evidently resident in several towns of the Punjab and Gujerat, and was more feasibly a trader than an official by occupation.

When the Mughal army took Balkh in 1646, a copy of Fani's *Diwan* was reportedly found in the library of the ruler of Balkh, Nazir Muhammad Khan. An ode in praise of this ruler offended Shah Jahan, who accordingly removed the poet from office at Allahabad, from where he retired to his native Kashmir, where he spent the rest of his days. Vans Kennedy aptly urged that the *Dabistan* author says he was at Surat (well to the south) in 1647, which does not geographically agree with the reported career of Fani.

While Erskine was lax in registering any connection between the Sipasis and the *din-i-ilahi,* Vans Kennedy made a slight improvement in this direction. He observed that Akbar's "religion" included veneration of the sun and the planets, a feature which he attributed to Zoroastrian influence (p. 270). Much has been written and conjectured about this subject since, and the research of Sir Jivanji J. Modi served to spotlight the formerly neglected *Dabistan* reference to the correspondence between Akbar and Azar Kaivan. Modi's 1932 article on Kaivan and his disciples was much more sympathetic and discerning than Erskine's damning critique, though still curtailed in its perspective by certain orthodox Parsi views. With regard to less orthodox inferences, the present author finds it impossible to agree with Modi's suggestion that Farzaneh Behram the elder authored the *Dabistan,* though it is not impossible that some pages in it emanated from that knowledgeable source.

If Erskine had grasped that there was a connection between the veneration of light in the *din-i-ilahi* and the ishraqi tradition (which he knew only as a simplified Sufism), he would have logically had to retract his denial of historical values in Sipasi literature. As it was, his non-comprehension of which values aided significant cultural progress serves as a warning against interpreting both history and allegory according to the canons of a strait-jacket historicism. It was not merely that the Akbarian empire was conceivably superior to the British sequel, but rather that philosophy in its wider dimensions cannot be made to fit piecemeal facts haphazardly surviving on paper.

Readers will have grasped by now that my own approach is radically different to that of Erskine and others. The philosophical approach need not be at variance with scholarship, though British scholars should currently endeavour to clear away former constraints in interpretation, much as British philosophers require to make due departures from old-fashioned empiricism. Since I myself am British, I have no hesitation in asserting such necessities. Many other countries have failings in exegesis, but one may only properly extend such critique to one's own country or ethnic grouping. It would of course be possible to extend these considerations to Europe and America, though some Continentals take the view that Anglo-American standards are separate from mainland Europe. This being so, here I can only stress to both British and American scholars and philosophers that thorough efforts be taken to ensure that no relapse to former insular standards be allowed to occur. This does not entail any absence of critical faculty when necessary, but rather a correct use of that faculty and the addition of more empathic qualities of approach as required. Historicists should not neglect the factor of meaning; at the same time, enthusiasts of meaning should take great care not to become absurdly ahistorical, since this results in its own specific maladies of confusion. If scholars neglect such finer points, then philosophers must make up the deficit.

APPENDIX 3: ISHRAQIS AND THEOSOPHISTS

In his *History of Zoroastrianism* (Oxford University Press, 1938), Dastur Maneckji Dhalla made a very inaccurate conflation which requires due correction. Describing the Sipasi (=Kaivani) philosophers as "Parsi Yogists," he described the Parsi members of the Theosophical Society as their "modern successors" (p. 508). One of Dhalla's accusations against the Theosophical Society was that it had "caused several members of the (Parsi) community to drift towards a growing fondness for occult mystery" (*ibid.*). This reflects Dhalla's commitment to orthodox standards, despite his criticism of ritual in Zoroastrian tradition. As a high priest of his community, Dhalla expected due subservience from his co-religionists. In misrepresenting the Kaivanis, his priestly view of Zoroastrian tradition as a whole can be very substantially questioned.

In his biased account of the Kaivanis (*ibid.*, pp. 464 ff.), Dastur Dhalla evidenced an ignorance of the ishraqi tradition that was strangely similar to that of the British historian William Erskine (see Appendix 2). Dhalla was unable to improve upon his predecessor in affirming that Sipasi teachings were based on "the earlier doctrines of Sufism and developed under Hindu mystic influences," and more specifically "Yogism," in his view. This was a particular stigma in priestly eyes, one considered to sully the purity of the Parsi faith beyond all reformist tolerability. The point is that the Kaivanis were not concerned with representing orthodoxy of any sort, but such heresy is never tolerable to bigots.

Dhalla was evidently indignant that some Kaivani works were alleged to be translations into Persian of Pahlavi books written in the Sassanian era. He remarked that the Persian treatises *Kheshtab, Zardusht-Afshar,* and *Zindeh-Rud* "mostly reproduce" Greek philosophy as preserved in the Arabic tradition, hence proving their pseudo-Pahlavi nature. It was lost upon him that, as Zoroastrian *ishraqiyyun,* Azar Kaivan and his circle were primarily interested in Greek philosophy as preserved in the Arabic philosophical tradition, rather than in Mazdean scripture and ritualism, the more justifiably since the Greek heritage was tangibly assimilated to a noticeable extent in authentic Pahlavi literature that mirrors the Sassanian interest in Greek science and cosmology. A clear Zoroastrian precedent for interests in Greek thought was not, however, sufficient to extend the intellectual horizons of phlegmatic ecclesiastics, who were quite content with their neglect of Greek and related matters of heretical thinking.

The Parsi members of the Theosophical Society, rapidly expanding in India from the mid-1880's onwards, were as ignorant of ishraqi matters as Dastur Dhalla. They affirmed that Azar Kaivan had been the last Parsi adept, and that with his death "the mysterious key to hidden truths was lost." This assumption of loss ignored subsequent developments extending to Sarmad and after; instead, the Theosophists asserted that only "occult science" could explain the allegorical teachings of Zarathushtra that were mentioned in the *Desatir* and *Dabistan*. It was declared that the founders of the Theosophical Society had acquired "a master-key that opened the hidden knowledge of all religions." This belief imitates Kaivani perspective, but as Dhalla (for once) pertinently notes, the Theosophical Society comprised an "eclectic system drawing its materials mostly from Hinduism and Buddhism" (*ibid.*, p. 503). The key to ishraqi lore was definitely not in the hands of Blavatsky and Olcott, whatever other talents they may have possessed.

The zeal of Henry Olcott and other Theosophists for the perpetuation of ritual is well known, and in pronounced contrast to Kaivani perspectives. The Theosophists even sought to vindicate the traditional Zoroastrian ceremonies by creating allegorical (or pseudo-scientific) interpretations to explain their relevance. This gained them the approval and support of the conservative Parsi religionists. The Parsi Theosophists affirmed that they were attempting to defend Zoroastrianism against innovations of the reformist party, a declaration which caused them to be regarded in conservative eyes as "the pillars of faith and the guardians of the edifice of ceremonialism" (*ibid.*, p. 504). It is understandable that Dhalla, as a reformist, should have reacted to the

Theosophists, but much less understandable that he chose to conflate them with the Kaivanis in defiance of the actual evidence. The allegorical interpretations in Kaivani literature have a totally different significance and intention; their whole context is one of sidestepping orthodox norms, not supporting them. That Olcott expressed a predilection for the *Desatir* is no proof that he understood its contents and context, which he evidently did not. The real significance of Kaivani literature was lost upon both traditionalists and reformists like Dastur Dhalla.

Olcott's "occult science" glorified magian ritual in the fetishist manner so curiously typical of Occidental lovers of the arcane. The so-called esotericists are more accurately to be classified with the exotericists, but such points are lost upon those who cannot discern elementary priorities.

Since the Parsi Theosophists were taught by Olcott to meticulously preserve their rituals in the hope of discovering their true meaning, it was perhaps inevitable that they maintained that Avestan prayers, "however unintelligible, were the most efficacious owing to their occult significance." This was bulwarking mysteriosophy with a vengeance. "Every single sentence conveyed an occult meaning" (*ibid.*, p. 505) was the gist of this determined attempt to preserve the exoteric at all costs to intelligibility.

Owing in part to the myopic conflation of ishraqis with exotericists by a Westernized sacerdotalist, I do not subscribe to the inapplicable description of Sohravardi Maqtul's philosophy (*hiqmat al-ishraq*) as Theosophy, not even in terms of the "Oriental Theosophy." This description has been employed by Henry Corbin and other scholars. Phenomenological myopia is a fitting companion for the exoteric; if the blind lead the blind, doubtless both will fall into the nearest pit of truncated meaning. A greater sense of historicity and meaning demands that due distinctions be made in so many directions that were neglected by Corbin.

The Arabic word *hiqmah* means wisdom, and even in its extension of *hiqmah ilahiyya,* is not equivalent to theosophy but to "divine wisdom." *Ishraq* is another word altogether, and not susceptible to postage stamp compression without due loss in meaning. Essentially it means "illumination," though "Oriental" is an acceptable variant if the full range of significations is grasped in this respect.

There is one last point in which the Parsi Theosophists may actually have been correct, a point ignored by Corbin and repudiated by Dhalla. The Theosophists expressed an incredulity towards the orthodox idea that metempsychosis had formed no part of Zarathushtra's teaching. The dasturs and other conventional Parsi scholars strongly opposed the Theosophical insistence that metempsychosis was an appendage to the Gathas. They relied upon Iranist scholars of the West (virtually all Christians) in support of the orthodox standpoint, and vociferously asserted "that in no period of the religious history of Iran was metempsychosis ever hinted at in the remotest form." They also rebutted the Theosophical interpretation of "one or two passages" allegedly torn from context (*ibid.*, p. 508).

This is one instance of dogmatic assertion that has been proven wrong. Not only did the Manichaeans hold views equatable with transmigration, but dissident trends like the Mazdakites of Sassanian Iran have also been strongly implicated in this worldview (see Shepherd, *Minds and Sociocultures,* Appendix 1). It may yet prove distinctly premature to insist that transmigration beliefs did not antedate the Sassanian era; in the face of later developments, this would seem extremely unlikely. The Kaivanis definitely did believe in transmigration, though they did not interpret orthodox scripture in this respect, unlike the Theosophists. Metempsychosis is a subject that has very frequently been exposited and reported without due clarification (on this, see Shepherd, *The Resurrection of Philosophy,* chapter seven).

INDEX OF NAMES

About the author:
Kevin R.D. Shepherd was born in 1950, and has been engaged in an extensive private research project since 1977. He is the founder of the Intercultural Research Centre of Anthropography, a non-political educational project which was initiated in November 1984 upon completion of his manuscript *Meaning in Anthropos: Anthropography as an interdisciplinary science of culture*, which now awaits publication. Anthropography is a new science of culture conceived and promoted by the author in a polymathic sense of commitment.

Anthropography covers philosophy, the social sciences, the human sciences, natural science, and the history of religions. It is both scientific and humanistic. Anthropography here extends well beyond current dictionary definitions; the geographical distribution of mankind is given a polymathic focus that does not obscure intrinsic evolutionary dimensions.

Anthropography does not stress mere polymathy as an antidote to over-specialized studies, but is concerned to indicate the priorities that should govern a comprehensive curriculum.

The interdisciplinary strategy of anthropography takes particular account of the heritages of non-Western peoples. The European heritage is also covered, but not at the expense of Asiatic contributions. The author is currently working upon a series of books which has a cross-cultural relevance to Western, Islamic, Jewish, Indian, Chinese, and other culture-groups.

His first book *Psychology in Science* (Cambridge, 1983) was an unusually forthright essay incorporating a support for the ecological emphases of the Club of Rome, an acknowledgment of Eastern alternative thinking, and a critique of scientific materialism and relativism. He defines himself as being primarily a philosopher, a stance readily apparent in his *The Resurrection of Philosophy* (in press).